*Positive Thinking Works!*
*Demarre McGill*

# A FATHER'S TRIUMPHANT STORY

Raising Successful African American Men

In Contemporary Urban Times

BY

## DEMARRE MCGILL

ISBN: 0988874911
ISBN: 978-0-9888749-1-6
Library of Congress Control Number: 2013916390
Demarre McGill, Chicago, IL

# DEDICATED TO

*My Mother and Grandmother*
*Mary Ann McGill*
*and*
*Laura Bell Scott (Hargrow)*


*Ira Carol's Mother and Grandmother*
*Eccorena Lake*
*and*
*Loretta Edwards*

# TABLE OF CONTENTS

# ACKNOWLEDGEMENTS

O n February 28, 1998, I began the task of writing the story of how my wife, Ira Carol and I raised our sons Demarre and Anthony to be successful men. At the time, Demarre was twenty-two, and Anthony was eighteen-years-old. Both had accomplished many of their short and long-range goals, and received many honors in their chosen field of study–music. I did not know that fifteen years later, I would still be working on this project. There were many long stretches of time when I did not write a word, or muster a single thought about the book.

Many family members, friends, musicians, or other people we met asked, "How did you raise such talented children?" "What did you do to raise two positive and talented boys?" These questions always motivated me to pick up my pen, and write on any piece of paper I could put my hands on. The notes on these scraps of paper, old envelopes, and notepads, eventually found their way into a document on my old Dell, Compact, eMachine, Gateway, Averatec, Toshiba, and other computers. A huge thanks to my wife Ira Carol, mother of Demarre and Anthony, whose words are italicized in this book. The constant encouragement, the many readings, and suggestions she made were indispensable. Most importantly, Ira Carol, thanks for being a great mother to our sons. A big thanks to my brother James, whose poetry is second to none. The computers James gave me through the years allowed me to record my thoughts in an organized fashion. Thank you to my sister Grayphenia (Gray), who spent many hours motivating me, reading my drafts, and telling me old stories about our life in Mound Bayou, Mississippi and Memphis, Tennessee.

Family friend, Dr. Sharon Hicks-Bartlett, was also a primary motivator. After discovering that I was writing, she encouraged me through her calm but forceful talks, and her harsh tones each time she discovered I was not writing. I owe a lot to Sharon, and without her constant inspiring suggestions, comments, her reading and editing, I would not have completed this project.

I am indebted to the numerous family members, friends, schools, teachers, neighbors, and arts organizations for providing a strong extended family that kept Demarre and Anthony safe, and contributed positively to their growth and development. Special thanks to Authors, Janis F. Kearney and Erin Goseer Mitchell for all the great advice they provided me.

Thank you Demarre and Anthony for being my sons, for your humanity, and your lifelong desire to be positive contributors to society through your words, music and actions. You guys continue to amaze not only your family, but people around the world. Stay focused and keep playing the music that makes all of us happy.

# FORWARD

A s parents, we would never send our children out without a coat to face the bitter cold and wind that aptly describes a typical Chicago winter. We would dress them well against the whipping Lake Michigan gusts. From head to toe we would safeguard them against the deleterious effects of winter's fury. Yet, everyday many parents send their children into the world ill-prepared and poorly cloaked against the emotional, social and societal woes that threaten their spirits and lives. By the time children enter kindergarten they need already to possess their first layer of armor against negative influences and emotional assaults, stereotypes and low expectations that the world will, to varying degrees, hoist upon them. When we send our children out, they should be ready to engage the world; they should be eager to learn all they can; and, they should be supported by parents who are their best advocates. *A Father's Triumphant Story*, is about the art and craft of parenting and how we can prepare our children to navigate within an increasingly discordant world so that they can accomplish whatever the heart desires.

This book details the joys and real world challenges of rearing two extraordinarily successful African American males from childhood to adulthood on the South Side of Chicago. That alone is an unimaginable accomplishment that far too many parents will never realize for reasons that are both inside and outside a parents' control. In these pages, a father shares his parenting wisdom and strategies for focusing on matters that we can control. It is a tale from which every parent should learn.

In these pages we meet the McGill brothers. As a long time family friend, I have met them and soon after meeting them one is likely to find herself wondering who are the parents of these talented and articulate young men. Mind you, I'm not referring to interacting with them now. At present, they are poised, polished and professional young, adult African American men at the zenith of their respective careers. I'm talking about when Demarre, the older brother, was a young teen and his brother, Anthony, was barely into the double digits. They were then just as they are now—just younger versions of themselves. Upon first meeting the brothers it is evident that they exude a confidence, comportment and courage that is unique. The brothers were not then, nor are they now average in any way.

These two brothers are wise and responsible; they are every parent's wish for their children. That both brothers also occupy enviable, principal positions in the world of classical music, a field with a noticeable dearth of African Americans, make their story a testament not only to their incredible tenacity and hard work, but also to the parents' investment in their children that commenced the moment each son drew his first breath outside the womb. This tale of parenting includes concrete lessons about emotional strength training, which feeds and fuels the mind, body and spirit of our children in the ways of the world. How can children navigate the many twists and turns they find in the myriad environments they will encounter?

I have engaged the brothers in conversations when they were young and have witnessed firsthand their development and observed the application of the parents' successful child rearing strategies. There is an adage that goes something like this, "Behind every good man is a good woman." I'd like to rephrase that aphorism to this certainty: Behind every Demarre and Anthony, stands exceptional parents or guardians and a network of positive mentors whose consistent wisdom, support and guidance has encircled that child as he journeyed through life's trials and tribulations.

I have observed the McGill parents for numerous years and during that time we have embarked on many long, ongoing discussions about parenting. Demarre and Anthony do not exist in a vacuum. To fully appreciate the life these young men have carved for themselves, one must take note of the parents who shadow them. Their sons' accomplishments are rooted in a family history of community, perseverance, and an abiding faith in the unlimited possibilities for a better future. Demarre and Anthony personify the outcome of remaining committed to family history and its values. The sons' awesome successes stand as incontrovertible evidence of their indefatigable determination to transpose their heart's yearning into a reality. There is no doubt about it. The McGills have reared two exceptional human beings.

Successful child rearing is not an accidental occurrence. Good, decent, responsible human beings do not raise themselves. There is an art and craft to parenting; thus, it came as no surprise to me that the McGill parents are both artists. Artists make something out of nothing; they move from vague idea, barren palette or blank page to creating beauty, to ultimately begetting something the rest of us can enjoy. In *A Father's Triumphant Story*, Demarre McGill, in full partnership with his wife, Ira, reveal the art and craft of their parenting. They share their game plan of principles and strategies for rearing successful children in contemporary urban times. We follow the author as he deconstructs the art and craft of parenting and inspires us, the reader, to take on the task of rearing productive, talented children.

The tale of two young African American brothers from the South Side of Chicago, both of whom have already made their mark in classical music, is a story that deserves telling. How did these two young men penetrate the classical music world, a world that can feel culturally and financially prohibitive to many? This book is about how any committed parent, regardless of where they live or how they earn their living, can and must focus on the important matters and on those things that reside directly within their control. While most of us are not artists or have an art background as the McGill parents, the principles espoused in this book remind us that we need not be artist to succeed. The art and craft of parenting can be taught and learned. A child arrives without any instructions and no guarantees of what she or he will become. We know from our own upbringing that the road will be replete with twists and turns. Still, as parents, we are called to do the work—the most important job ever required of us.

Modeling what we want for our children, living our values and working hard is real parenting. The McGills practiced a style of child training that avoided the ineffective approach that some parents adopt when they tell their children to "do as I say do." Such parents want good outcomes without good input. The McGill parents modeled what they knew would be winning skills and traits. They left no wiggle room; they closed the gaps to prevent falling through the cracks of ambiguity. They lived what they taught because they recognized that our children are always watching and studying us. Our children can spot the inconsistencies between what we say and what we do. The messages they gave their children were compatible with the behavior they modeled. From the beginning, their expectations for their children remained high, as did the expectations they held for themselves as parents. As often heard on the South Side, they "walked the walk, and talked the talk." When values, beliefs and work ethic are compatible and in alignment with our behavior and deeds, children come to understand their place in the world and their responsibility as good human beings.

Throughout *A Father's Triumphant Story*, we read how the parents augmented their sons' protective layers of self; we hear how they fortified their sons, smoothing out the dents and kinks that maturation inflicts. It is an ongoing process that parents cannot afford to take lightly. Deeply committed parents must believe unconditionally that their child can do whatever the child desires-no holds barred. Children need sage guidance and relevant tools to negotiate their way through whatever life presents them. Equally important, they must possess a drive that can withstand setbacks. These tools consist of far more than the tangible attributes we all assume are necessary for success, such as education and training. The toolkit must also contain numerous intangible qualities, such as tenacity, responsibility, civility, and exceptional valor. The toolkit needs, what I call, the Jackie Robinson mien, where even in the face of incredible odds, one does not lose sight of their dreams and goals, where giving up is never an option. It is possessing a skill that Martin E.P. Seligman calls "learned optimism." Learned optimism is the ability to see in every situation, every experience, the positive elements that can continually move us forward rather than derail us and end our progress. I do not know if the McGill parents have read Seligman. Regardless, they possess those characteristics of learned optimism and practice a parenting style that includes equipping a child with an array of accoutrements, talents and dispositions to navigate relatively unscathed in the sometimes tousled terrain of living a life.

What is unique about this book is its simple wisdom and commonsense principles. But do not be deceived. Often the simplest things are the hardest to accomplish. Raising children today is difficult work. Rearing successful young people who know and believe in their bones that they possess all that they need to embrace the world fully, children who know that they inherit an obligation and responsibility to constructively contribute to this world, is a Gargantuan challenge that requires, at minimum, actively devoted parents and ideally, a network of supportive adults upon whom the child can rely. This is our tasks as parents and responsible adults invested in the survival of our future.

This is not easy work. Some parents want to be their child's friend; some even avoid saying "No" for fear the child won't like them, or that such words will hurt the child's feelings; some parents enable the child by taking the child's side in all matters. This, the McGills will tell you, is not parenting—at least not the parenting path that leads to raising successful children. With love, confidence, guidance and an unyielding abundance of positive support, the McGills reared their sons with the end in mind. That is, they parented without losing track that the goal was to produce independent, proud and strong adults. They gave their children what we all need to give to our future. They gave them, to paraphrase Jonas Salk, roots and wings. Roots to be able to stand firm and remember from whence they have come, and wings to soar high and know that inherent in every fiber of their being they possess all that it takes to do whatever they want in this life. For them, the sky really is the only limit.

If we are fortunate, we have had positive role models from whom we can pattern our parenting. Most of us however, have no such models, or perhaps we have been bequeathed a mixed bag of parenting skills, some of which are good and some that are not. Many of us can recall a time when a parent meted out a discipline that we felt was unjust and our response, uttered under our breath, was something like; "I will never do that to my child." At the time, we did not know what to replace "that" with; and, as adults, many of us are still trying to figure out what to replace that with. In reality, no matter how much we resist, we often end up repeating what was done to us because our skills to do the contrary are in short supply or nonexistent. What we all need to acquire are strategies and principles that work and serve as the building blocks of tools needed to raise and protect our children well.

In heartwarming and humorous stories and proven "how-to lessons," *A Father's Triumphant Story: Raising Successful African American Men in Contemporary Urban Times*, is an indispensable guide on what our children need. They need us. Our time. Our attention. And, our unconditional love openly and frequently expressed. The art and craft of parenting is within everyone who brings forth life. That innocent newborn who looks to us for its every need is the job we sign up for when we become real parents. A real parent is one who nurtures the child, provides guidance, supplies all that the child needs and some of the child wants. Real parents keep a vigilant eye on the child's psychosocial development and make the necessary adjustments when needed. Not every parent conveys to their child that the child is the single most important person in the parents' life. Real parents never miss such opportunities. Even in the midst of a major challenge with a child, it is important that children know that they are loved.

While not everyone will be—or wants to be—an accomplished classical musician like the McGill brothers, everyone has the same obligation to be all that he or she can be. That so many do not fulfill their potential is a fault that we as a society must accept. It all starts in the home, but home does not exist in isolation. These are challenging times. Not everyone faces the same neighborhood challenges in parenting; not all families share the same employment protection against fluctuations in the economy or can send their children to public magnet schools. Such differences influence parenting and signal to us just how much will be demanded of us to buttress our children against the pushes and pulls on their mind, body and spirits. All children are at risk and some are at greater risk than others. McGill's 25 Principles remind us of our need to protect our children by showing us how to focus on what's really most important in rearing successful children against great odds. This book does not ignore the harsh realities that too many parents face in certain communities as they struggle to keep their children safe, engaged, focused, and positive about fulfilling their goals and dreams. All parents, according to the McGills, must have a game plan, a set of strategies for transcending negative spaces and places. Parenting is one job where winging it will not work.

Even if one masters the art and craft of parenting, we know that life holds no guarantees. The maiming and murder of children is far too frequent in these times. Yet, successful parenting is non-negotiable. Without equipping our children with protective skills, tools and dispositions, without encouraging their talents, we are sending children out into a blizzard without a coat. How do we surround our children with protective gear so that the odds of making it are in their favor? *A Father's Triumphant Story* tells us how Demarre and Anthony McGill's parents accomplished this task. And, the results are now in. The world can see the McGill parents' greatest works of art. Soak in the wisdom; apply the principles. Relish the words on rearing exceptional human beings. Then listen to the results of extraordinary talent from two renowned classical musicians, two African American brothers who grew up well on the South Side of Chicago.

**Sharon Hicks-Bartlett, Ph.D.**

# DEMARRE MCGILL

*Demarre Lavelle McGill, Principal Flutist of the Dallas Symphony*
*Orchestra. Photo courtesy of Demarre L. McGill.*

*Anthony Barrone McGill, Principal Clarinetist of the Metropolitan Opera Orchestra. Photo by David Finlayson.*

*Demarre, Anthony, and Mr. Rogers. Courtesy of the Fred Rogers Company.*

# CHAPTER ONE

## BROTHERS DEMARRE AND
## ANTHONY MCGILL

On February 25, 1994, Mr. Fred Rogers, of *Mister Rogers'*
*Neighborhood*, the highly regarded children's television program, invited some special guests to the neighborhood. Musicians,
eighteen-year-old Demarre Lavelle McGill on flute, and his
fourteen-year-old brother, Anthony Barrone McGill on clarinet,
performed on the show. Mister Rogers, known for his friendly,
warm-hearted nature, and the beautiful days he created in the

1

neighborhood for his millions of viewers, had this to say about his young visitors following their amazing musical performance:

> Those young men, they spend their time doing healthy things. Things that don't hurt anybody. In fact, their music helps people. They practice as they play, and they make life better by doing it. I'm very proud of them for what they do, and how they do it, and who they are. *(Mr. Fred Rogers, Episode 1674, Mister Rogers' Neighborhood, 1994)*

As proud parents, Ira Carol and I concur with Mister Rogers. Demarre and Anthony have spent their young lives working hard and passionately to master whatever endeavor in which they invested their time. We have witnessed their progress, their tenacity, and can attest to how their hard work has paid off for them.

Long before they were the renowned classical musicians they are today, they were young African American males growing up on the South Side of Chicago. Their experience on *Mister Rogers' Neighborhood* was huge. It motivated them to work even harder on their music.

Well before they were out of their teenage years, Demarre and Anthony had accomplished many of their short and long-term goals. Throughout this time, they received numerous honors in their pursuit of becoming successful classical musicians.

Millions of adults and children saw two well-groomed and well-dressed African American teenagers from the South Side of Chicago playing extraordinary classical music on a national television program. Chances are some of these viewers were motivated to become musicians because of this.

Their performance on *Mister Rogers' Neighborhood* with Alan Morrison, pianist and classmate of Demarre, place them in the company of some of the best musicians and artists in the "neighborhood." As a means of inspiring young children to strive for excellence, Mister Rogers was known for inviting famous people to be guests on his show. Yo-Yo Ma, Tony Bennett, Andre Watts, Hilary Hahn, Ella Jenkins, Van Cliburn, Lynn Swann, and David Copperfield are just a few of the hundreds who appeared. To this day, Demarre's and Anthony's performance on this world-renowned show remains one of the highlights of their careers.

The art, science, or methods of raising children in today's troubled world is a monumental task. Some say that raising African American boys is even more daunting. Don't believe the hype, or what you see daily on the television and Internet news shows. It can be done. Families across America are doing just that. Some in the news media believe there are no, or few African American boys being raised to be men who contribute positively to society. I believe this is a myth.

As of June 23, 2013, Ira Carol and I have been married forty years and are proud to say that we raised our sons to be successful men. Our love, support, guidance, and their hard work, positive mental attitude, and quest to be the best in all of their endeavors, have helped Demarre and Anthony gain worldwide acclaim in the classical music arena.

In September of 2013, Demarre began his first season as Principal Flutist with the Dallas Symphony Orchestra, and is co-founder of *Art of Élan*, a successful chamber music organization based in San Diego, California, whose goal is to "expose new audiences to classical music, and to enrich the cultural life of San Diego..." *(artofelan.org)*

Demarre is also a member of *The Myriad Trio*, a chamber music group comprised of Demarre, Brian Chen (viola), and Julie Smith (harp).

Anthony is currently the Principal Clarinetist with the Metropolitan Opera Orchestra in New York, and is a member of the Schumann Trio. Anthony, violist Michael Tree, and pianist Anna Polonsky founded the Schumann Trio in 2008. Michael Tree is also a founding member of one of the world's greatest musical ensembles, the Guarneri String Quartet. Anna Polonsky is an out-standing pianist who is well respected in the classical music field. Anthony's solo career is growing rapidly. He has performed with many of the top classical musicians in the business, and continues to receive requests to perform with major orchestras and ensembles across the country and the world.

On January 20, 2009, an estimated two billion people around the world saw and heard Anthony perform at the inauguration of President Barack Obama. What a fantastic emotional explosion my mind experienced when Anthony informed Ira Carol and me that he was officially invited to perform at the inauguration of the first African American to be elected President of the United States of America. This is an outstanding accomplishment for a young man from the South Side of Chicago.

The Joint Congressional Committee on Inaugural Ceremonies (JCCIC), invited Anthony, Yo-Yo Ma, Itzhak Perlman, and Gabriela Montero to perform a few minutes before President-elect Barack Obama was administered the Oath of Office. This world-class quartet performed a new piece called *Air and Simple Gifts,* written by Grammy award-winning American composer, John Williams. Anthony's inaugural performance will be a part of American and world history forever.

Anything is possible in The United States of America. Parents must constantly believe their children can be whatever they want to be. Let your children know that their dreams and goals can become realities.

On June 15, 2009, Ira Carol and I celebrated our thirty-sixth wedding anniversary by inviting one hundred of our best friends and relatives to a dinner party at Governor's State Golfing Center, located in University Park, Illinois.

My younger brother James, wrote and recited a prayer before the food was served. The following are James's thoughts about being connected:

*President-elect Barack Obama being sworn in as the 44ᵗʰ*
*President of the United States. Photo by D. McGill.*

# *CONNECTED*

*Father, years ago you brought forth for us a young boy from a small town in Mississippi and named him Demarre, and a young girl from Chicago with the name of Ira Carol.*
*They were CONNECTED.*
*You brought forth a black man from Kenya and a white woman from Kansas.*
*They were CONNECTED.*
*You spread the McGills from the South to the North and from the West coast to the East coast.*
*We are CONNECTED.*
*You gave us Barack and Michelle.*
*They are CONNECTED.*

*On a cold January day in 2009, the world listened as Anthony McGill played the John Williams composition, "Air and Simple Gifts," and then Barack took the Oath of Office.*
*They were CONNECTED.*
*The world watched in awe and was*
*CONNECTED.*
*We understand that what flows from one connection to another is and will always be, YOUR LOVE.*
*From the infinite past to the unpredictable future, your love flows and connects us all, no matter who we are or where we came from.*
*We experience such joy and happiness when your love explodes in the past and the present and we feel our connection to you and others.*
*We thank you for all our connections and all the connections possible for us in the future as you bless us constantly with the flow of your love.*
*The McGill family thanks everyone here tonight and we pray that future connections are revealed to you and that your connection to us...is...and will always be eternal, with much love, flowing from the source.*
*Father, we thank you for this food we are about to connect with.*
*Amen!*
*James McGill, June 15, 2009*

James knew what he was talking about when he said, "We are connected." Sometimes we don't realize these connections exist until a future conversation or meeting.

My family's connection to President Barack Obama goes back to November 20, 1993, over twenty-years-ago. On this date, The Monarch Awards Foundation of Xi Nu Omega Chapter of Alpha Kappa Alpha Sorority, Inc., presented its Eleventh Annual Monarch Awards Gala. The sorority's program was entitled, *A Tribute to Black Men*. This organization was founded in 1908 on the campus of Howard University, and has a membership of over one hundred thousand college educated women, and over seven hundred fifty chapters across the world. The sorority's motto is, *Service to All Mankind*.

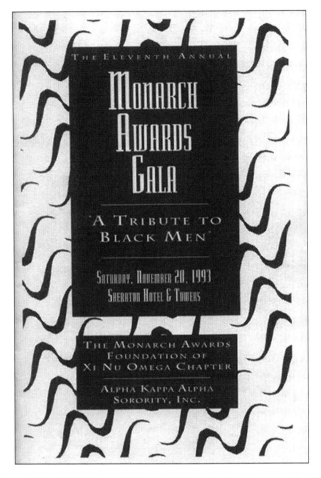

*Cover of the 1993 Monarch Awards Foundation program booklet.*

The awards program honored thirteen African American men who exemplify and practice its motto. One of the men being recognized was thirty-two-year-old Barack Obama, who was honored for his "Public Service."

Along with the thirteen men, one teenager was honored. Eighteen-year-old Demarre Lavelle McGill received the "Outstanding Youth" award. No one knew that at age eighteen, Demarre would be sharing a stage with the future President of the United States. Demarre's and Anthony's connection to Barack Obama shows us that in one way or another, we are all connected.

*We are all stitched together in a universal pattern of life. Each person's stitches dissecting and intermingling with others and forming an integrated pattern created by God. Ira Carol McGill*
In September of 2009, Anthony was featured on *Gramophone Magazine's*, *ENCOUNTERS* page. The title of the article was, *Making the Connection-Clarinetist Anthony McGill on how cellist Yo-Yo Ma helped him dig deeper into music's meaning.*
The following quote is Anthony's description of how his connections to Mr. Ma changed the way he interpreted music:

Meeting Yo-Yo Ma changed my life twice. Years ago (2001) I gave a concert in Tokyo of Messiaen's Quartet for the End of Time alongside Mitsuko Uchida, Mark Steinberg, and Yo-Yo Ma. This was one of the most special concerts I've ever been a part of.

You usually have to think about hearing, never mind creating feelings in music. But Yo-Yo expressed pure emotion through his playing. His sound actually went inside me, as if someone could play with their soul and then reach into you and touch that same part of you. That's how it felt. Every shake of his vibrato with the left hand, I felt. In rehearsal, Yo-Yo made a little comment during the solo clarinet moment. 'What are you seeing? What do you imagine, when you're playing this? An abyss? A huge canyon? Is there darkness? Go home and think about it.'

I'd played pretty well, but went back to the hotel and looked at the music. Then I imagined the music. I imagined the space the music inhabited. And the next rehearsal, I played and imagined—he looked over and gave me this happy smirk. It was like, 'Yeah.'

BARACK OBAMA
Public Service

In the final, climatic buildup to November's general election, one of the most important local stories managed to go virtually unreported: the number of new voter registrations before the election hit an all-time high. And the majority of those new voters were black. The most effective minority voter registration drive in memory was the result of careful handiwork by Project Vote! At the head of this effort was a little known 31 year old African American lawyer, community organizer and writer: Barack Obama.

Mr. Obama received his Bachelor of Arts from Columbia University and his law degree from Harvard Law School. He became the first black president of the influential Harvard Law Review.

Mr. Obama is currently an attorney with Davis, Miner, Barnhill & Galland. He specializes in civil rights litigation and commercial transactions relating to the construction of low-income housing and redevelopment of low-income communities.

Mr. Obama is currently completing a book on race relations in America and Africa, tentatively titled Journeys in Black and White, to be published by Random House in Spring 1994.

*Barack Obama's page from the Monarch Awards program booklet.*

All of that changed my ideas of what I could reach towards as a musician. It showed me that I could go deeper. That the imaginative capacity for what your brain does before you play in expressing music is one of the most important tools. What you think about can really affect what the listener feels. Take away the instrument and what remains is a mental and emotional connection with the listener. The clarinet just helps me use that. Fast-forward

DeMarre Lavelle
McGill
Outstanding Youth

This 18 year old musical sensation is already in his sophomore year of college at the prestigious Curtis Institute of Music in Philadelphia. He will receive his Bachelor of Music in 1996.

He began his training at the Sherwood Conservatory of Music in Chicago and also attended the Tanglewood Music Center.

This accomplished flutist has received first place honors in the following competitions: NAACP ACT-SO, Flute Talk, Society of American Musicians, Illinois Young Performers, Chicago Youth Symphony Concerto and Interlochen Arts Camp Concerto.

Mr. McGill is indeed a role model for young, aspiring musicians.

*Demarre McGill's page in the Monarch Awards program booklet.*

eight years and three days before the programme for Barack Obama's inauguration was announced, I got a call from Yo-Yo's manager, saying he'd like to play a concert with me and wondered if I was available on January 20. When I called back, she revealed that the concert would take place at the inauguration of President-elect Obama! So there I was, in rehearsals with Yo-Yo again, digging deep and thinking back to his lesson of eight years earlier.

The John Williams piece gave me the chills, and there's a moment when you hear the main melody, low, simple and soulful. That moment opens up the world, and thinking as Yo-Yo had taught me, I realized it also

*Anthony and Cellist Yo-Yo Ma at President Barack
Obama's January 20, 2009 inauguration.*

opened the sense of the possibilities of the moment, of
what was happening with this man.

Growing up as a black kid on the South Side of Chicago,
and playing classical music, I felt that music right away, on so
many levels. And all that was thanks to Yo-Yo Ma. *(Anthony
McGill, Gramophone Magazine, September 2009)*

Demarre and Anthony have received many important awards
during their music careers, but the Avery Fisher Career Grant is
one of the most important ones. The Career Grant is a component
of the Avery Fisher Artists Program, which was established in 1974
by the renowned inventor and philanthropist Mr. Avery Fisher: "to

give outstanding instrumentalists significant recognition on which to continue to build their careers...These musicians, who must be U. S. citizens or permanent U. S. residents receive these awards based on excellence alone." Mr. Fisher donated millions of dollars to assist in the development and training of musicians, and to improve the viability of arts organizations. In addition to the recognition they received, Demarre and Anthony were awarded a one-time grant of $15,000 each. This money, given early in their professional music careers allowed them to repay some of their music related obligations. Manhattan's Lincoln Center for the Performing Arts administers this program, which is recognized as being, "one of the most prestigious in the music world." A "Recommendation Board" chooses recipients of the award. Musicians do not audition, and are not informed that they are being considered for it. Many of the world's greatest and most well-known musicians of our time have been awarded the Avery Fisher Career Grant. Some past recipients include: Violinists Ani Kavafian, violinist Joshua Bell, flutist Marina Piccinini, violinist Tai Murray, violinist Wendy Warner, clarinetist David Shifrin, clarinetist Richard Stoltzman, violinist Pamela Frank, pianist and conductor Ignat Solzhenitsyn, and my sons. Anthony received the Career Grant in 2000 and Demarre in 2003.

The McGill brothers are the only African American siblings to ever win this award. Our dedication to raising our sons, and the love and support we provided, gave Demarre and Anthony a solid foundation to be whatever they wanted to be. Their fortitude, dedication, and determination paved the way for them to become two great musicians and highly successful young African American men.

Mr. Avery Fisher said, "Musicians of outstanding ability are such an important part of our culture. But they are like flowers that must bloom at a particular time." For a plant to grow and bloom, it needs nurturing. It needs water and light to make food to sustain itself and produce beautiful flowers. We can also apply this idea to raising children. For children to develop, grow, and blossom into positive and successful adults, they also need water and food to nourish their bodies. Unlike plants, which make their own food through photosynthesis, adults must provide infants' and children's emotional and intellectual nourishment needs externally. Children also need loving parents, or other love ones to nurture and raise them through the infancy, childhood, and adolescent stages of their lives. They need people like you.

Ira Carol and I knew that in order for our sons to be successful, we had to provide them with a positive home environment, the best schools, and great teachers. With our guidance and support, and the assistance of family and friends, brothers Demarre and Anthony survived the South Side of Chicago and now are successful African American men.

Raising children is difficult and time-consuming work, and should be the number one priority of all parents. Millions of parents are using their own techniques, as well as some of the principles my wife and I used to raise successful children. There was no guarantee that our sons would survive to be who they are today, but we knew that if we dedicated our lives to "raising them well," their chance of being successful would be enhanced exponentially.

*Polaroid photo of Mr. Rogers, Demarre, Anthony,*
*and Alan Morrison. McGill family photo.*

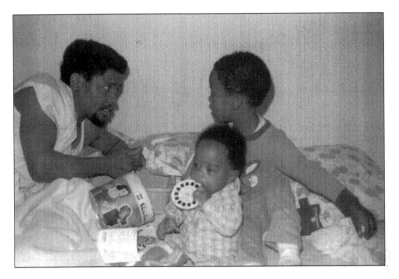

*Me, Demarre, and Anthony in 1980.*

# CHAPTER TWO

## MCGILL'S 25 PRINCIPLES

The following are twenty-five principles Ira Carol and I used to raise and teach our sons. I am sure there are many other principles, guides, or teaching tools parents use, but these are the ones we concentrated on while raising our sons on the South Side of Chicago.

Some of you may recognize that your parents used these same principles during your own upbringing. Understand that what works for one person or family may not work for you. Sift through the principles and choose ones that you feel comfortable with. I am sure that years from now or sooner, you will be writing your own principles–adding to the never ending keys parents across the world use to raise successful men and women.

### Key Principles For Raising Successful African American Men

1. Look at your child and say, "I Love you," at least once every day. Because of the stress put on you by outside forces, and even by your own son or daughter, you may not want to say these three powerful little words. Tell your child, "I love you," regardless of how you feel at the moment.

2. All human beings need to be loved and touched. Give your child a strong hug and a kiss on the cheek, every day.

3. Don't be a drop-off parent. Be there during the parent and teacher meetings, music lessons, basketball games, swimming classes, and all of your child's activities. Children get satisfaction out of knowing their parents are sincerely concerned about their well-being and success while they are involved in activities, whether outside, or inside their home.

4. Before and after your child is born, use every opportunity to teach. While in his mother's womb, his brain is functioning and responding to sounds. Do not think your child is incapable of learning at this young age. He is listening and learning.

5. Praise and compliment your children equally. Avoid sibling rivalry by not comparing siblings. They are individuals, and should be judged on their own merits.

6. Spend quality time with your child every day. Help him with homework assignments, and watch positive programs on television together.

Take him fishing at the local lake, to a little league baseball game, museum or a live concert or theater performance. Play old-fashioned board games and sports with him. Search your local newspapers to find free opportunities. Many museums have free days, and cultural centers have free activities and concerts. These fun and educational experiences will create an everlasting bond between you and your child.

7. Remove the television and computer from your child's bedroom. Place them in a common area of the house to monitor their use. Use Internet filters, or parental controls to block out sexual and violent content on the computer. Travel to faraway places with your child–by "surfing the web."

8. Find the best teachers. Good teachers will motivate your child and inspire him to want to learn. If necessary, seek the advice of friends, relatives, or other teachers, and understand that you should be your child's number one teacher.

9. Know your child's teachers, friends, and the friends' parents. Get telephone numbers and home and email addresses. Periodically communicate with them to establish an extended family of concerned parents, teachers, and friends.

10. Pick up your child after school if possible. This helps to ensure the child's safety. A photo of your child holding your hand while carrying his book bag will be an everlasting family treasure.

11. Recognize behavioral changes in your child, investigate causes, and take immediate action when necessary. In other words, "nip it in the bud." This prevents the issues or problems from growing into larger ones that might be difficult to manage.

12. Read to your child every day. Take him to a library and buy plenty of books. Visit used bookstores where you can find some low priced hidden treasures. You might also find that great classic at one of your local flea markets–for less than one dollar. During the summer months, explore outdoor book fairs, and don't neglect the indoor ones during winter. If possible, invest in a digital reader, they are cheaper than you think. Some are priced less than one hundred dollars. There are many Internet sites where you can download free books. Don't forget to buy some cloth books before your child starts to walk or talk. Most importantly, when he learns to read, have him read to you.

13. Find creative ways to reward your child for his accomplishments. Take him to see his favorite movie. Surprise him with a new pair of gym shoes, a new basketball, or a new book. Allow him to roam the aisles of a toy store and pick one or two of his favorite toys (within a certain price range).

14. Talk to your child. To teach, you must talk to him. Two-way communication is vital for you to get to know your child, and for him to get to know you. To understand what's going on in your child's mind, you must also be a good listener.

15. Don't let money be an issue. Your son's and daughter's success is worth every dollar. Take the necessary action to secure funding to support them. Take out a second mortgage if possible, or get a part time job. If you have a special skill, barter your service to pay for the music, dance, swimming, gymnastics, or science classes. Ira Carol once painted graphics on each side of Mr. Montgomery's school bus. In exchange, he transported Demarre from home to school and back for a full year.

16. Be at home with your child, especially during the infant and childhood stages of his life. A positive and loving home environment can be a natural classroom for teaching. When a babysitter is needed, use family members or friends who share the same positive values as you.

17. Write encouraging letters or notes to your child. During the early years, these letters and notes can be used to teach reading and writing skills. In a short period of time, your child will be reading and writing to you. As he gets older, these letters and notes can be used to show your love and to motivate him to succeed.

18. Teach your child to establish goals early in his life. Ensure that the goals are written down and posted in the home, and on his computer and mobile phone. Let him know that goals can be changed periodically. Give your sons and daughters a special reward or treat each time they reach one of their goals.

19. Discipline your child when necessary, but don't ever use physical or mental violence as a disciplinary tool. Just as you found creative methods to reward your child for doing the right things, when it comes to discipline, be just as creative.

20. Save your child's artwork and other writings. Frame his drawings, paintings, and poems. Display them on the walls of your home. Displaying your child's creations helps to increase his self-esteem. Save all photographs and videos of your child. These gems will bring many smiles and tears of joy later in life.

21. Don't allow your child to say *I can't*. Teach him how he *can*. Constantly try to instill in your child's mind that he can reach all goals if he works hard and believes in himself.

22. Mental workouts are necessary for your child to succeed in school and the physical ones are just as important. Go to the park and run. Play catch with a football or softball. Take long walks in safe areas. Sign him up to play organized team sports. This physical activity helps boys and girls develop strong bodies and minds.

23. To provide healthy foods and drinks for your child, and to identify harmful ingredients found in many popular foods, read ingredient labels found on the packaging of all grocery store foods. Limit the amount of sodium and sugar in your child's diet. Try not to eat or drink foods containing high fructose corn syrup, or other sweeteners like brown sugar syrup. Some food companies changed the name high fructose corn syrup to corn sugar. Many researchers have found these sweeteners to be harmful to humans. Foods with high amounts of trans fats should also be avoided. Avoid foods that are classified as genetically modified organisms (GMO). Do whatever is necessary to avoid childhood obesity by being a healthy role model for your child.

24. Teach your child to respect others. Teach him to have positive values. Teach him the meaning of the verse, "Do onto others as you would have them do unto you."

25. Be a positive role model for your child. Be his loudest cheerleader—at his school's holiday program, little league baseball game, music competition, or at the family bowling outing. Let him know through your actions that you care and want him to succeed, no matter what the endeavor. Parents who are raising a young child should begin to use these principles early in his life. Don't wait until he reaches a certain age—some principles can be used on the day he is born.

These twenty-five principles are not all encompassing, and I am sure, if you are serious about "raising your children well," your own principles will evolve. Your list of principles might even be more extensive than the ones listed here. Use whatever tools and guides that work for you.

Throughout this book, I sometimes used the words *he* and *him*, and the words *Raising Successful African American Men* are found in the title. It is important to remember that these principles can be used to raise all children, regardless of gender, race, ethnicity, or social class. The key is to use these principles every day to, "raise them well."

*In 1998, I bought this button for $10 at an*
*antique store in Memphis, Tennessee.*

# CHAPTER THREE

## MY SOUTHERN ROOTS

I was born in Mound Bayou, Mississippi on March 6, 1950, in a house my father, James McGill, built. Daddy was a self-taught carpenter who built many of the houses in Mound Bayou, a small town about one hundred miles south of Memphis, Tennessee on old Highway 61. We used to joke that Mound Bayou was so small that if a person held his breath upon entering the town, by the time he exhaled he would be outside the city limits.

After my mother moved our family to Chicago, Illinois in 1963, I was ashamed to tell classmates and friends that I was born in

Mississippi. If anyone asked, I always answered, "I was born in Memphis, Tennessee." At the time, I was even embarrassed that my birth certificate listed *Black* as my race. During this time, *Black* was offensive to many people. *Negro* was the acceptable term during the 1950s and 1960s. The person who completed the boxes on my birth certificate would probably turn over in her grave if she knew that *Black* would ultimately become the norm in describing the race of descendants of African slaves living in the United States.

In December of 1887, Isaiah Montgomery and his cousin Benjamin T. Green, purchased eight hundred and forty acres of land for seven dollars an acre. They named this area Mound Bayou after a large Native American mound located in the area. Although some say that Mound Bayou is the first officially chartered all Black city in the United States, a few other cities also make this claim. On February 16, 1898, Isaiah Montgomery and twenty-nine other residents of the unincorporated village of Mound Bayou, petitioned A. J. McLaurin, the governor of Mississippi, to get the village incorporated as an official city. The governor approved the petition in a proclamation issued on February 23, 1898. In 1912, the village was given the status as a city by then Governor Earl Brewer. At the time of incorporation, there were one hundred eighty-three inhabitants of the new city. Isaiah Montgomery held the positions of Mound Bayou's first Mayor and Justice of the Peace. Montgomery finally had a place he could officially call home.

Montgomery was born into slavery on May 21, 1847 on a plantation owned by Jefferson Davis, the "Father of the Confederacy." Montgomery's father, who was owned by Jefferson Davis, taught him to read. Isaiah Montgomery eventually became the private secretary and office attendant to Joseph Emery Davis, the brother of Jefferson Davis. This relationship provided Montgomery with access to the Davis library, which he used to further his knowledge of history, math, and many other subject areas. *(Information from Portrait of a Black Town, THE VOICE, Volume 4, Number 8, Steve Williamson, July, 1971)*

*Isaiah Montgomery's home in Mound Bayou, Mississippi.*

For many decades, Mound Bayou was a city known for educating its youth, many of whom sought educational opportunities in colleges and universities in the North. One such person was Dr. Theodore Howard, a famous medical doctor from Mound Bayou who originally worked as a physician at Mound Bayou's Taborian Hospital. When I was two-years-old and living in Mound Bayou with my family, Dr. Howard sewed four stitches into my scalp to close a large cut and to stop the bleeding after a newly sharpened hoe fell on my head. My mother told me that my father, before sitting down under a tree to rest after chopping weeds in the cotton field next to our home, leaned his hoe against a low hanging branch. One of the other children who was playing in the area bumped into it. The hoe fell down and the blade struck me on the head. Tape marks can still be seen above my right eye. This long indentation seems to get deeper as I get older. This is probably caused more by the buildup of fatty tissue on my face rather than by age.

*Uncle Jim Robinson (on the right) and friend in front of Taborian Hospital. McGill family photo.*

Taborian hospital was built in 1942 by the International Order of Twelve Knights and Daughters of Tabor, an African American fraternal organization. The hospital is still standing, but has been closed since 1982. Weeds are growing on the roof and vines have crept up the old red brick walls. Fortunately for Mound Bayou, in July of 2013, workers began to rebuild this historic hospital. Taborian will soon reopen as Taborian Urgent Care Center.

I was amazed when at age thirty; I discovered that Dr. Howard lived in a large ranch house on 83rd street in the Chatham community of Chicago, four blocks from where I was living. This man was always a mystery to me, for after he stitched me up back in 1952,

26

*The house in Mound Bayou, Mississippi*
*where my siblings and I were born.*

I never saw him again. I used to imagine the many stuffed animals rumored to be hanging on the walls of his house. It was said that Dr. Howard made many trips to Africa where he went on safaris and brought back the heads of large animals. I don't know if this was true or not, but it was fascinating thinking about this mystery man and the mounted trophies in his home. I wondered if the Robin Williams movie, *Jumanji*, was made in Dr. Howard's basement.

My oldest sister Grayphenia, we call her Gray for short, said, "MuDear and Daddy raised hogs when we lived in Mound Bayou." MuDear is my mother, Ms. Mary Ann McGill. Gray told us how every Fall, Daddy and other men in the community slaughtered hogs and prepared the meat that we ate all year long:

> Daddy attached a heavy wooden board to the house at the roofline. This board was parallel to the ground and extended out about three feet. A hog was killed, and to

drain the blood, a rope was tied to its hind legs and hung from the corner of the house. The entire carcass was then dipped into a large black metal caldron filled with boiling water containing lye, a harsh chemical.

The hot water and the lye burned the hair off the hog. The hairless hog turned white after it was removed from the caldron. Daddy then used a large knife to cut open the belly of the hog to remove the intestines, and all of the internal organs. *(Grayphenia Bayles)*

Daddy didn't throw the intestines away, or for that matter, he probably didn't discard any parts of the hog. They were cleaned, cooked and eaten by us. Today we call the intestine delicacy, chitterlings, or better yet, in that old southern vernacular, chitlins. Go to any grocery store in the African American community and you will always find some frozen or loose chitlins. The hog meat was cured in an old-fashioned smokehouse. We feasted on this meat for months.

Gray recently told my brother and me that MuDear and Daddy also raised chickens while living in Mound Bayou. Baby chicks were ordered and mailed to my parents' home. They were packaged in containers similar to egg cartons. Gray said, "Usually, half of the baby chickens died while in transit. Once the chicks arrived, MuDear kept them under a bright light to keep them warm. We always had chickens while in Mississippi."

There is an old saying, "If you don't know where you came from, you won't know where you're going." As a means of exposing our sons to my southern roots, Ira Carol and I, took them to Mound Bayou and to Memphis, Tennessee when they were five and nine years old. They were shown the small house my father built and where my brothers and sisters were born, other homes built by him, and the large field next to the house where cotton once grew during my early childhood. Daddy even won a cotton-picking contest in this *cotton field next-door.*

I showed them the vacant lot down the street from the house where my siblings and I were born. This lot once held my grand-mother's (Mama) house and store she owned with her husband. Mama was married four times. The store was connected to their living quarters. A screened-in breezeway separated the store from the house. There was a large pecan tree, an apple tree, fig tree, and two peach trees in the back yard. If any of us got hungry, all we had to do was go out back to the garden, or pick up fresh fruit or nuts that occasionally fell from the trees.

We visited the hill where my brothers Barrone (Roni), James, and I played when MuDear visited Mound Bayou after we moved to Memphis. During these trips "back home," Roni and I ate the sun-baked soil that curled up like potato chips after a moderate rain and a few hours of the hot Mississippi sunrays. We broke the sun dried soil chips from the hard ground and ate them. My sons gave me a funny look when I told this story, especially after I said the hard-ened soil tasted like chocolate candy. Is this the reason I love to eat chocolate today? Could this be the Indian Mound for which Mound Bayou was named? I have yet to find the answers to these questions. Demarre and Anthony seemed fascinated by their narrated tour of my poor southern roots. By taking my sons *back in time*, letting them see where I came from, and comparing that to where our family is today, my wife and I attempted to instill in their minds the thought that there is no limit to what a person can achieve in life. We con-stantly told our sons they could be whatever they wanted to be if they continued to think positively and work hard.

I remember Mama, with her thick reddish stockings rolled up just above her knees, and the old country looking flowered dresses she used to wear. Mama was a dark skinned woman with sharp cheekbones she attributed to her Native American ancestry. Although there are African American families in the United States whose ancestors were Native American, I don't have any scientific evidence of this being the case with Mama.

*May 1, 1932 photo of my grandmother, Laura Bell Scott (Mama),
Uncle Jim, and my mother, Mary Ann (MuDear). McGill family photo.*

Mama told us weird stories when we were children. One I vividly remember was when her husband put a voodoo spell on her. "I almost died from some strange voodoo spell," Mama said. Gray recently told me: "I was with Mama when she found a shoebox under the wooden steps leading to the breezeway of her house. The box contained a small handmade doll, which had pins stuck through the head, bird feathers, some hair, and other unrecognizable items." Mama believed that finding the shoebox saved her life. Mama also found a matchbox that contained strands of her hair. At the time, these stories were fascinating and scared the *living daylights* out of me.

These stories are probably responsible for Ira Carol and I not entering the back room of a voodoo shop down in New Orleans in 1973, shortly after we were married. We were walking along a street

*My mother's Mound Bayou High School graduation photo.*
*MuDear is standing next to her teacher. McGill family photo.*

in the French Quarters and noticed a small voodoo shop situated between two old unpainted buildings. Adventurous as we were back then, after a short discussion, we decided to enter this shop. A scary looking female greeted us. She was wearing a long floor length dark brown and white dress. The scarf wrapped around her head and neck, was made of the same material as her dress. We walked around this store looking at the small human-like skulls and other small bones on the windowsills. The large colorful paintings hanging on the walls seemed to show dark skinned people in various positions, some dancing and others sitting on the ground.

This woman reached down and pulled back a dark cloth curtain that covered a doorway to another room in her shop. She invited us to follow her to the rear so we could, "See some more interesting things." Ira Carol and I looked at each other, and immediately turned around and headed toward the exit door, trying desperately not to trip over our feet. After this experience, I think we returned to the hotel room to catch our breath, which we thought was about to be taken away from us.

In late May of 2010, my brother James, sisters Gray, and Tonisene (Toni), and I visited Mound Bayou for the first time in many years. Gray's daughter Krishna, my niece Essence, and nephew Demitrios, travelled with us to Mound Bayou. We were in Bartlett, Tennessee to attend Essence's high school graduation ceremony and decided to visit the place of our birth. We had dinner with Mrs. Annyce Campbell and her daughter Chris. Eighty-seven-year-old Mrs. Campbell has lived in Mound Bayou her entire life, and was a good friend and neighbor of my mother and father. They were also classmates at Mound Bayou High School. Mrs. Campbell, who was elated to see us, said, "No one ever comes back to Mound Bayou once they leave."

The tears running down her face told us that her emotional expressions were sincere. This was a fascinating visit for all of us. Before we sat down to eat dinner, Mrs. Campbell told stories about our family's early days in Mound Bayou. She blessed the food with a heartwarming prayer. I recorded Mrs. Campbell's prayer with my phone.

> All mighty God, we come to you this moment with a grateful heart full of thanksgiving for allowing this portion of the family to be reunited on this day, at this time. In a place Lord, if I had been the one to try and make this happen, I feel that I would not have been able to do it. But I thank you Oh Lord for these children that care and love me so much.
>
> I thank you dear God for having them to remember and come home to just see about me. To be with me sometime and let me see them. When I know they are

well, then everything is well with me. Oh God, thank you for this family, and thank you dear God for the way these children are being reared.

But dear God, thank you for your constant care and guidance. Their home training and their love of humanity have blessed us all to be home together.

Lord, I feel that they are just as happy to be with this portion of their family as I am to have them. They are, and I know they are, they are happy to be home. Oh God, you have been so good to us. Just don't let them forget their home ground. Thank you, Jesus.

Mrs. Annyce Campbell
May 23, 2010

After we paused to wipe the tears flowing down our cheeks, we feasted on fried and baked chicken, pork chops, greens, cornbread, green beans, macaroni and cheese, cornbread dressing, and homemade cakes and pies. An hour after we finished stuffing ourselves, the adults were still sitting at the dinner table listening to tales of the past and laughing until our jaws hurt. Mrs. Campbell was still crying and laughing with us.

We eventually left the kitchen and packed ourselves into two vehicles. We drove around the tiny city. The church my family belonged to, and one my father helped build, is still being used. We visited the small cemetery and took pictures of my grandmother's headstone, situated next to a large unmarked casket shaped concrete structure. I wondered if this was Isaiah Montgomery's gravesite.

Gray took photographs of Isaiah Montgomery's house. This huge red brick mansion, built by a former slave, has also been abandoned for decades, but must have been the talk of the town back when Montgomery lived in it. The visit to the place of my birth felt like a spiritual experience, but seeing so many young unemployed African American men standing around, the rundown hospital, and the lack of any form of industry, was sad. This was an awe-inspiring trip for my family and me.

While living in Memphis, MuDear worked at Trojan Luggage Company. Daddy worked at the Army Depot, but he was in and out of our lives. MuDear struggled to provide for us.

The people on our block helped us, and Mr. Smith, our next-door neighbor, occasionally brought us a four feet high bag of outdated white bread he picked up at the Wonder Bread factory. It seemed like the huge brown bag contained a hundred bags of smashed white bread. Some of the bags containing the individual loaves were ripped open, but this was no problem for five hungry kids. Peanut butter and jelly spread over the wrinkled slices was one of our favorite treats.

In 1960, Daddy departed Memphis and started a new life in Chicago. After MuDear left Memphis to reunite with Daddy, Mama received government surplus cheese and powdered milk through a program designed to help poor families. The cheese was bright orange, shaped like a large elongated rectangular brick, and seemed to weigh about five pounds. My grandmother would always say, "Boy, don't eat too much of that cheese. It'll stop you up." Because of my many painful experiences in the bathroom, I clearly didn't take her advice. Nowadays when I eat cheese, thoughts of my grandmother enter my mind. I am very conscious of the amount of cheese I eat, and its color. No more orange cheese for me.

The powdered milk was dehydrated cow's milk, packaged in a large brown cardboard box. Mama made liquid milk by adding water to the powder, and she also made clabber with it. She called this concoction buttermilk, but I never saw any butter in it. Mama mixed the powdered milk with water in a large pickle jar and allowed this mixture to curdle on the kitchen table. The soured mixture of powdered milk and water resembled modern day yogurt. I don't remember how long it took for the milk to sour and thicken, but when the clabber was ready, Mama cooked a large skillet of yellow corn bread.

We mixed the clabber with broken pieces of corn bread, added a pinch of sugar, and filled our stomachs. James recently said, "To add flavor, I mixed Kool-Aid with my clabber." The cornbread was delicious. Many times I sprinkled sugar on the hot cornbread, spread some butter on top, and imagined that I was eating cake. Man, that was good eating! The clabber had a thick but smooth texture in the mouth, and the cornbread added a roughness and flavor that made the mixture go down easier. This was not one of our favorite meals, but it filled our stomachs. I recently asked my Aunt Geraldine about clabber.

Geraldine, affectionately known as Aunt Jelly, was married to my mother's brother, Uncle Jim. Aunt Jelly's family owned a large farm down in Duncan, Mississippi. They owned cows, hogs, and grew their own vegetables, apples, peaches, pecans, and black walnuts. She told me that her family milked the cows and allowed the milk to sour or curdle overnight, and then churned it to make butter. This is probably the reason Mama called her clabber, buttermilk. Our home was not filled with steak and lobster, but the love my mother, grandmother, aunt, and uncle showed us, filled our hearts, minds and stomachs.

## *HOT WATER CORNBREAD*

*Hot water cornbread, a poor man's meal*
*Requires so little, just some cornmeal for starters*
*A little bit of flour, salt, and garlic powder*
*All the ingredients to make it quick*
*A pinch of sugar added, if you wish*
*Stirring and mixing, fix it up fast*
*Complete addition to make a meal last*
*Boil some water, and sizzling oil*
*Add to the dry ingredients and mix in a medium bowl*

*Heat some oil in a skillet on top of the stove*
*Pour in the cornmeal mixture to make several patties,*
*Fry it on one side then flip to the next*
*Until you have hot water cornbread to add to the rest*
*Hot water cornbread takes a skillful hand to make*
*It's a delicacy of sorts that enhances*
*A bowl of chicken soup, vegetable stew*
*Mustard, collard, turnip greens too*
*Spaghetti if needed and a pot of string beans*
*Hot water cornbread, a poor man's bread*
*Something so simplistic, so easy to make*
*Treasured by...only a few*
*Ira Carol*
*11-3-96*


During this trip down memory lane, we visited the large grey stone church on Springdale Street located near our old house in Memphis. We talked about the poems all the little children had to memorize and recite during Easter Sunday, Christmas, and other church programs.

Behind the church, in a large open field where we played football and baseball, stood a large Black Walnut tree. This tree produced some of the tastiest nutmeats ever grown. Roni and James, and I developed a system for harvesting the walnuts from this tree. We didn't wait for them to ripen naturally on the tree and fall in late September and October. We threw sticks or dead tree branches into the tree and hoped that when they fell back to earth, walnuts would follow. We were always successful; for it seemed that each year the harvest was greater than the previous one.

Before taking the walnuts home, my brothers and I used the same sticks to remove the thick lime green hulls from the hard walnuts. This process caused our hands to become dyed a greenish yellow by the natural liquid dye found in the unripe hulls. It

*May, 2010 photo of my family's home when we lived in Memphis, Tennessee.*

took weeks for the dye to wear off our hands. Our clothes were also spotted with the dye from these green walnuts. After removing the hulls, the walnuts were taken home and allowed to dry and ripen in the attic. We ate walnuts all winter long. These were not the relatively soft shell English Walnuts that are light brown or tan in color. When ripe, Black Walnuts are dark brown. The shell is thick, and we used a hammer to break them to get the tasty treats out. We could have waited for the walnuts to fall from the tree and dry naturally, but by then, we would have had to share our harvest with the other kids in the neighborhood. My brothers and I always decided to get a head start on everyone else. Because I love to eat black walnuts, peanuts, and pecans, my mother once said, "Boy, you must be a reincarnated squirrel." I never doubted my mother. For about three months, I even had a gray squirrel as a pet when I was sixteen-years-old and living on 88th Street on Chicago's South

Side. MuDear eventually talked me into releasing him because of her rabies fears, and the fact that she did not want a squirrel in the basement of our house any longer.

I don't go out looking for walnut trees anymore, although I know the location of several I found during some of my fishing trips to the Kankakee and Illinois rivers. I smile when I look back on my childhood. All of the unsupervised outdoor activities my brothers, sisters, friends, and I participated in were so much fun. We played marbles, spinning tops, football, baseball, and took long walks into other neighborhoods in the area without having to fear anyone. We explored nature in forest areas near our home and the Memphis City Zoo.

After finding whole pecans in a wooded area near Mr. Ambrose's house on Hubert Circle, one of the questions we asked was; "How did the pecans get there?" We never found any pecan trees growing in the area. Some of the boys thought the ghost who lived in the forest dropped them. We eventually agreed that the nuts were probably dropped by birds, or brought into the area by some other animals.

At night we gathered to listen to the children crying in the forest where we played. We all tiptoed to an area near the rear of Mr. Ambrose's house and squatted down. After a few summers, we finally discovered the strange sounds were coming from cats that lived in the area.

We sometimes sat on the edge of old eroded Cypress Creek, which flowed through the neighborhood. All the kids in the area called this stream *The Bayou*. The water always looked muddy from our shoreline vantage point, ten feet above it. Collecting balls from the creek as they slowly floated by was lots of fun. After heavy rains, this was dangerous because of the softened natural shoreline, but some of the bravest boys seemed to take pride in their risk taking. Luckily, none of our friends drowned while we lived in this area.

I told Demarre and Anthony how we played *Tarzan* in the wooded area near where the pecans were found. The long thick vines were cut and pulled from the trees near the zoo and dragged to our play area on Hubert Circle. The vines were tied high in the trees, which fronted an open area. After climbing onto one of the big branches of our favorite trees, and grabbing the vines, we swung out like that ape-man on television, screaming until our feet hit the ground.

This was great fun until Roni swung out and the knot holding the vine slipped. Roni crashed to the ground and his rear end landed in a dug out pit where we broke any glass bottles we could find. We thought he was knocked unconscious until he opened his eyes. The thick blue jeans MuDear bought us probably prevented serious cuts to his rear end. Roni limped home and stayed inside until the next day, when we were once again swinging in the trees. This incident was good for about two weeks of continuous laughter.

Although we occasionally got into fist fights with our friends, most of the time we were looking for that next outdoor adventure, and laughing at each other. We didn't have much money, but we sure did know how to have fun, and how to laugh.

We played our dangerous war games like children today do. The big difference was we used old bicycle inner tubes and rocks instead of guns and knives. One cut was made across the circular inner tube so the ends could be tied to two strong branches high in a tree. Branches that formed a big Y were chosen. This weapon looked like a gigantic slingshot, which we also made. After filling our pockets with rocks, we climbed the tree and tied the tube to the branches. After we placed a rock into the center of this over-sized slingshot, it was stretched back as far as possible and then released. The rock flew like a missile toward the enemy, who were usually my brothers, or some of the other boys from the neighborhood. Fortunately, no one was killed or seriously injured during our medieval wars.

We made kites out of thin paper from the cleaners up on Springdale Street, or brown Kroger sacks from the grocery store near Uncle Jim's house. The grocery sacks were thick, but if no other paper was available, we used them. The tail was made of any old rags we could find at home, and the kite string was purchased at Mr. Johnson's little store on the corner of Springdale and Hubert Circle streets. The frame was made of straight flexible dried out tree branches. What a thrill it was when after running with those kites for seemingly miles, they caught an updraft and soared like eagles in the sky. It was fun watching the tails zigzag in perfect harmony behind the homemade kites. These activities were totally natural to us, and things learned during these outings remain with me to this day.

One of our favorite meeting places was the hard, bare earth in front of Mrs. Jones's house, where we wore out our blue jeans at the knees shooting (playing) marbles. Before we left Memphis, my brothers and I gave our collection of over 1500 marbles to our friends. We were the best marble shooters in the neighborhood, and I wish we still owned them. They are probably worth a small fortune in today's collectables market.

The most popular marbles in our collection were called Cat's Eye. They were beautiful transparent spheres with multi-colored centers resembling a cat's eye. The larger marbles were called hoakies, and were about two or three times the size of a regular marble. Some of the hoakies were made of steel. We called these steelies, and always kept them shining by rubbing them on our shirts or blue jeans. We seldom used these monsters. Shooting marbles was generally a boy's game, and one of my favorite outdoor activities. While the girls were playing hopscotch, jacks, patty cake, or jumping rope, my brothers and I were rounding up the other boys on Hubert Circle and playing some serious marbles.

To start the game, one of the boys used a hard sharp stick to carve a square into the ground. Sometimes a circle was used. The square was usually about one square foot in size. A four-feet long straight line was drawn about five or six feet from one of the sides and used as a starting point. This line was drawn horizontal to one of the sides of the square. Each player placed an equal number of marbles into the square. We never started by putting our prettiest marbles in. All the old, ugly, chipped ones went in first. From the starting line, each member took turns launching a marble with his thumb and index finger into the collection of marbles.

The beginning of the game reminds me of the initial break of an 8-ball pool game. To knock out as many marbles as possible, each player propelled his marble into the center of the square. We were allowed to keep all the marbles that came out. If our marble also landed outside the square, we could continue shooting. If it remained in the square, a turn was lost until another player inadvertently knocked it out. Our marble games sometimes lasted for hours, or until Mrs. Jones got tired of hearing our loud arguments and fights.

It seemed like the rules of the game were always changing, although they were established before we started playing. Shooting marbles was good, clean fun, and one of our favorite outdoor games. Every now and then the fun was broken when a ten-minute fistfight broke out. I vividly remember Herman hitting me in one of my eyes with his fist as a result of a marble related argument. That punch hurt and I saw stars for the next hour or two. Most times we continued the game with a few bruises here or there, but with friendships still intact. That blow to my eye ended my game of marbles for that day. These games were serious business, but fun for all of us. Each of us had our own strategy for winning the most marbles. The only problem was, we kept Mama and MuDear busy ironing those big blue jean patches onto the knee area of our jeans. I did not like those new patches. They stood out like a sore thumb on our old faded jeans. MuDear didn't like those holes in our jeans and wasn't about to buy new ones. She always kept an extra supply of patches, her iron and ironing board ready.

Many of our toys back then were made of paper, like the homemade kites we flew. Uncle Jim taught us how to make paper airplanes out of a single sheet of notebook paper. No glue, scissors, or balsa wood was needed, only several strategically placed sharp folds and we were flying paper airplanes that sometimes soared like birds. We made little paper hats that resembled old-fashioned army caps and marched around like little toy soldiers once we put them on our heads.

Our noisemakers were also made of a sheet of notebook paper. Again, with a few sharp folds, a triangular shaped noisemaker was made. We held the two outside corners of this paper toy, bent our arm back so that the toy was near our ear, and popped it like we were spinning tops, without releasing the tightly held corners. The interior section of the triangle shaped toy popped out and made a loud noise similar to the sound a small balloon makes when it pops. We popped this toy until the paper became too soft. Perhaps our favorite toy was a Duncan Yo-Yo. This was one of the most popular toys during the 1950s and 60s. It seemed like every boy or girl we saw was carrying a Yo-Yo. The difficulty was, we had to buy them. We never figured out how to make these toys, but I'm sure we tried. My sons were amazed when I bought them a Yo-Yo and taught them how to *walk the dog, rock the baby in the cradle,* and how to do the *around the world.*

The girls and boys played their separate games, but sometimes we played together. Some of my favorites were pop the whip, hide and go seek, dodge ball, croquet, and hopscotch. We also spent hours stretched out on the ground, looking for that one lucky four-leaf clover, hidden among the tens of thousands of three-leaf clovers growing in all the yards on Hubert Circle. No guns, no knives, no money, just great fun and a wrestling match or fist fight every now and then. We had some good, clean fun when we lived in Memphis, and played for hours, although when we arrived home from school, the first thing we did was our homework, and a few household chores. Mama and MuDear made sure of this. I also don't remember ever being absent when I was in elementary school, and only a couple days during my high school years.

My mother and grandmother always stressed the importance of doing well in school. If we used the word can't while in Mama's presence, she would immediately say: "Don't use that word around here! I don't want to hear you say, I can't again. You can do whatever you set your mind on."

## *YOU CAN*

*I can't change the way you think*
*I can't give you physical strength*
*I can't force you to keep going*
*I can't keep your creativity flowing*
*I can't study for you and*
*I can't make you believe in God*
*But I can help you discover*
*That YOU CAN!*
*Ira Carol, 2-16-10*

MuDear and Mama were two of the biggest influences in the lives of my siblings and me. These women did everything within their power to provide for our physical and mental needs. They taught us to always hold our heads high and to think positively no matter how difficult the situation. Mama and MuDear were two strong women in our lives. They contributed greatly to our growth and development as positive adults. Without them, I don't know where my siblings and I would be today. Ira Carol and I used some of the same techniques we learned from our parents, grandparents, uncles, and aunts, to instill positive attitudes and moral values in our sons. We constantly used Mama's quotes when Demarre and Anthony used the word "can't."

Parents, make a kite with your children. Take them to the park and let them run with it. Take a photograph of their smiling faces

*My great grandfather, Jim Hargrow, great grandmother, Alice Laster-
Hargrow, and my Uncle Jim Robinson. About 1940. McGill family photo.*

as the kite catches the blowing wind. Your son's and daughter's
inner emotions will soar like that homemade kite. Your emotions
won't be far behind and I guarantee that you and your children
will never forget this experience. Twenty years later when you talk
about the fun times you and your children had, don't be surprised
if a couple of tears start to form in the corners of your eyes. Tell
them stories about your childhood experiences. These memories
are what life is made of. Make them happen for your children and
cherish them for a lifetime. That bedtime story could be one of
your childhood adventures. Share them with all of your children.

Just like Isaiah T. Montgomery, who was born into slavery and
overcame major obstacles during his life, with the help of family and
friends, any child can accomplish his or her lifelong goals if he or she
receives the proper support and is willing to put forth the effort.

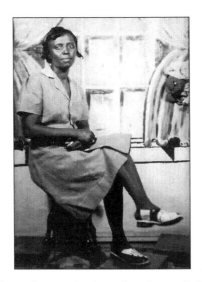

*June 9, 1942 photo of my mother's mother, Laura Bell Scott (Mama).*

# CHAPTER FOUR

## MY FAMILY'S MOVE TO CHICAGO

My father James always had good jobs, but was an alcoholic who gambled most of his money away when we lived in Memphis, Tennessee. He constantly came home drunk and fought MuDear. After he moved to Chicago, he worked in various jobs and eventually settled on doing small carpentry jobs whenever he could find them. I didn't know my father very well, and Gray told me and James that Daddy didn't spend much time at home with us, and had even more serious problems within his other Chicago family.

In 1962, MuDear traveled to Chicago to try to reunite with Daddy. This attempt at putting the family back together did not work, and MuDear decided to return to Memphis.

During the summer of 1963, Mama, Uncle Jim, Roni and James, my youngest sister Toni, and I, left Memphis to seek the rich bounty of the big city. MuDear and Gray had already relocated to Chicago, after Gray got pregnant. I was thirteen at the time and was initially both excited and apprehensive about moving. I envisioned Chicago as being paved in gold, but I still didn't want to leave my friends whom I had so much fun playing with.

Elaine, Sherry, Charles, Ricky, Peter, Robert, and Herman were some of our Memphis friends who watched us load the car and a small U-Haul trailer. They also seemed excited about the move. The colorful postcard images of Chicago were branded into my brain. I remember Mr. Fuller, who owned the white house on the hill, wrapping a thick strap around the Frigidaire refrigerator, lifting it onto his back and carrying it to the trailer. I wondered how any man could carry a large refrigerator on his back. We didn't own much furniture, so nothing was left behind.

Uncle Jim pulled the trailer behind his brown 1956 Chevrolet. We all were filled with excitement during the five hundred thirty-five mile trip north, but crossing that seemingly two feet wide bridge over the Mississippi River at Cairo, Illinois made us forget about Chicago. Traversing this narrow two-lane bridge was a scary experience, especially at night. I remember that first crossing. A large truck was approaching Uncle Jim's car after he had driven about two-thirds of the way across the bridge. A strange optical illusion caused me to scream because it looked as though the truck was in our lane and coming straight towards my uncle's car. Uncle Jim, in a loud manly voice shouted, "Shut up boy, you're making me nervous. Be quiet and go to sleep." I crossed that narrow bridge many times as an adult, until the government built the big, new, green steel bridge that stands today.

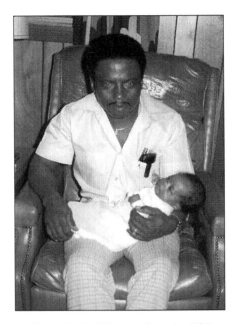

*Uncle Jim holding Anthony in 1979.*

Mama told us stories about the Ku Klux Klan in Cairo, Illinois, and how Blacks were targets of racism while driving through this small town. The route over the old bridge took us through downtown Cairo.

I vividly remember seeing a man's name and the words *Justice of The Peace* painted on a big sign in the front yard of one of the houses. Toni asked Mama, "What is Justice of the Peace?" She answered, "If a person did something bad, they would be brought to this house by the police, and be thrown in jail by the Justice of the Peace." He was the judge and the jury all wrapped up in one person. At this time in my life, this was scary stuff.

Between the old bridge and the racism stories, my brothers, sister Toni and I were ready to turn my uncle's old Chevy around and go back to Memphis. Our dreams of living in the big city called Chicago faded, and we wanted to get out of Cairo immediately.

*Aunt Jelly holding Anthony.*

We arrived in Chicago late on a summer night and were totally shocked when Uncle Jim drove under a viaduct at Cermak Road and Drake Street, into a dark unpaved bumpy road, which led us to Mr. Johnson's building on South Homan Avenue. We felt a strange eeriness as we passed a coal yard near a railroad track where people bought coal to heat their homes. The coal looked like small black mountains to me. To the kids who played in the tiny park across the street, this coal yard was like Chicago's Wrigley Field bleachers. If one of the children hit a Chicago made sixteen inch Clincher softball into it, this was an automatic home run. I even notched two or three homers during my play lot career.

One of the weirdest sights was the two-story grey stone buildings, which looked like stacked shoeboxes with about three feet of space between them. My family had always lived in one story single-family homes that my parents owned in Mound Bayou and

*My mother's first check stub she received after our move to Chicago. MuDear worked 72 regular hours and 8 holiday hours and made $104.95.*

Memphis. The front yards of these houses were tiny compared to the open spaces of the South. At this point, I was again ready to go back down to Tennessee.

Uncle Jim stopped the car in front of a building near the corner of 21st and Homan Avenue, and I remember Mama saying, "This is our new home." We all slowly wiggled out of my uncle's car, glad to be able to stretch our legs, but unsure about the new neighborhood.

Mr. Johnson met us at the front door and Mama introduced us. He was a large Black man with Asian facial features. The Johnson family was a large Catholic family who helped us feel comfortable in this new environment. Our second floor apartment was nice and spacious, and had a dining room and a kitchen. We had never seen a house like this, but quickly got used to it. We had great fun while living on Homan Avenue, from ice-skating in the streets, swinging on the monkey bars, playing basketball, and fist fights in the sandpit.

MuDear took a job as a nurse's aide at Mount Sinai Hospital after arriving in Chicago. Although it seemed like MuDear worked fifteen hours a day, she actually worked a regular eight-hour shift. She kept decent clothes on our backs, Buster Brown shoes on our feet, and plenty of food on the table. The 1962 blue Chevy Belair she bought looked like a Rolls Royce, and was handed down to me in 1970 after she bought a blue 1968 Chevy Impala. Although she worked full time during the day, MuDear went to night school and became a Licensed Practical Nurse. She looked beautiful in her new uniform, including the starched white cap. She was especially proud of the gold LPN pin she wore on her collar.

This woman was determined to be the best that she could be, and although Daddy was nowhere to be found, she and Mama did a tremendous job raising us. The examples they provided helped to mold my brothers, sisters and me into the positive individuals we are today. Her influence is still being manifested in her children, grandchildren, and great grandchildren living throughout this country.

Uncle Jim and Aunt Jelly also contributed a great deal to our family's survival. When my siblings and I were youngsters, my uncle constantly recited a poem to us. He encouraged us to memorize the short poem. I recited it to my sons many times during their childhood.

*If a task is once begun,*
*Leave it not until it's done,*
*Be the labor great or small,*
*Do it well or not at all.*
*(Author unknown)*

Uncle Jim died in 2005. He suffered from Parkinson's disease for many years before his death. Before he passed away, I spent a full week living with and assisting him. I did this to spend some quality time with my uncle, and to give my Aunt Jelly some rest. I told her to take a vacation, for she worked tirelessly, twenty hours a day taking great care of her husband. Aunt Jelly didn't take a vacation. She spent time at her daughter, Deanie's house. I told my Aunt I would not phone her unless it was absolutely necessary. Unfortunately, I had to call because of the problems Uncle Jim was having.

Mama was the disciplinarian in our household. She kept all of us in line by whipping us with a braided vinyl coated clothes-line, a rubber coated extension cord, or a switch from the Weeping Willow tree in the backyard of our Memphis home. This tree was huge. Many of the low-hanging branches touched the ground, and it was like being under a massive umbrella when we swept the branches back with our arms and played near the base of the tree. We were in our own little wonderland under this tree. Whenever Mama was thinking about giving us a whipping, she would say, "Boy, go out there and get me a switch off that Willow tree." We always came back with the smallest we could find. Mama didn't like this and usually made us fetch a bigger one. Those skinny branches hurt, and I'm sure they wept along with us.

My brothers, sisters, and I were not discipline problems, but every now and then Mama had to show us that she was the boss in this family. We sure did not like the whippings, but we still loved and respected our grandmother. Mama passed away in 1968 during my senior year at Farragut High School, located on the West Side of Chicago. I remember being at Allied Radio, where I worked after school, when a relative called to inform me that Mama had died. I cried all the way home. I truly loved my grandmother. She was with me, and my brothers and sisters every day of our lives. More than anything, this strong woman taught us to strive to be the best and to "do unto others as you would have them do unto you." I miss Mama to this day, and think about her all the time.

Although Mama was the major disciplinarian, one of the most memorable whippings was one I received from MuDear in 1964. I was an eighth grader at Spry Upper Grade Center on the West Side. MuDear had recently bought me a new winter coat to fight the cold Chicago winters. Spry was about one and a half miles from home, and I walked to and from school.

After leaving school one cold and snowy day, a classmate named Larry lit a cigarette when we were about three blocks away from the school. "Here man, you want some of this?" he asked, as he was handing me the cigarette. I said, "No way, I've never smoked before." This boy continued to ask if I wanted to take a puff from his cigarette. I reluctantly took the cigarette from his hand, and slowly lifted it towards my mouth. When I put the cigarette between my lips I saw a police car coming towards us. "That's a police car," I hollered. The sight of this car scared the heck out of me, and without thinking, I cupped the cigarette in my hand and placed my hand into my coat pocket, thinking the hand would prevent the cigarette from contacting the inside of the pocket. Well, it didn't work. My coat was smoldering although I didn't know it until we got within a few blocks of my home. Larry started screaming, "Your coat is burning, your coat is burning!" The cigarette had burned through the inside pocket lining of my new coat, and a hole could be seen on the outside of the coat. I thought I smelled something other than the cigarette burning, but I was too naive to realize that my new coat was smoldering. I panicked, took the coat off, and started beating it on the snow-covered ground.

I was glad the policeman didn't see me smoking. I thought he would throw me in jail, although I knew MuDear was going to kill me if she found that hole in my brand new coat.

I delayed going home and thought I could conceal the hole from my mother. When I opened the front door, she met me, and immediately shouted, "Boy, what's that burning smell?" I said, "Nothing." MuDear's nose started working overtime. She started pulling on the coat. She lifted my arms and found the burn hole. It was still smoldering around the edges. Wool coats burn forever, you know, and give off this strange pungent odor. Well, MuDear beat my butt big time.

*My mother, Mary Ann McGill.*

Three years went by before I tried to smoke again. I occasionally smoked during my last year of high school, while in college, and a couple of years after. The last cigarette I tried was at the Disneyland Hotel in 1974. I'm glad I got that out of my system, although MuDear almost beat it out of me back in 1964.

Although they are frowned upon now, whippings were part of the normal process of raising children back then. I should have listened to MuDear. One of her favorite sayings was, "A hard head makes a soft behind."

*Ira Carol and me.*

# CHAPTER FIVE

## THE MEETING THAT CREATED
## DEMARRE AND ANTHONY

O n March 5, 1949, I was born at Cook County Hospital in Chicago.
My mother was Eccorena Lake and my father was named Anderson
Lake Jr. According to my mother, my birth was not easy. Unbeknownst to
me, I was ready to come into this world backwards. I tried to enter walking or feet first. The medical term for this type of birth is breech. The doctor
had to turn me around. To further complicate matters, I was dropped on
my head shortly after being born. This incident ultimately became a family

*joke. My mother would occasionally say, "You ain't never been right since then."*

I remember my mother as being someone who could do no wrong. She was an African American woman who always had a very stately figure, although she gave birth to six children. I was the first born, and I vividly remember the births of all my siblings, especially my three younger sisters.

Like my husband and his siblings, our mother and grandmother raised us. Loretta Edwards gave birth to my mother when she was fourteen-years-old. My mother was the only child of my grandmother. The circumstance of Loretta's pregnancy is not completely known to our family. We only knew that my mother's father was much older than Loretta, and he was married.

There were no men in the immediate family during our upbringing. I vaguely remember seeing my father once when I was about nine-years-old. It was then that I realized that my mother's last three children had a different father than me.

Eccorena was an attractive lady we called Mama. She was a caring and kind individual and mother. As children, we loved to sleep with Mama, and she was always accommodating. My siblings and I were allowed to keep any pet we found or wandered to our door. We owned a cat named Blackie, a turtle named Leroy, and a mistreated dog named Slue Foot. We gave him this name because he hobbled along on only three legs. The fourth leg was always tucked under his body. Mama would help anybody who needed assistance. She never allowed anyone to mistreat us. She just loved to help people and animals. Our financial status was poor, but our home environment was rich with love. We were raised on Chicago's South Side. Our early days were spent at 4824 South Calumet Avenue. The apartment building where we lived was originally built to house six families instead of the eighteen separate living spaces (kitchenettes) the building owners illegally created. There were six kitchenettes on each of the three floors of this building.

We lived on the first floor. To enter the building we had to walk up a couple of concrete stairs. Framing the stairs were huge concrete blocks on each side. We called these blocks, stoops. My sisters, brother, and I spent many long hours, especially during the summer, playing and resting on the stoops. At the top of these stairs were two glass doors that had dark *and heavy wooden frames around them. Once through these doors, there were mailboxes and doorbells on the left and right. Directly in front of the entrance doors were six marble-looking stairs that led to another door. This door was always locked. Once inside, our home was small, but Mama made it comfortable for us.*

*Mama did her best to provide for us, but needed assistance from the government. I remember our family receiving public aid, or welfare as some called it. Welfare was considered a negative word in the community, but this assistance helped my mother and grandmother through the hard times we experienced. Ira Carol*

I met Ira Carol Lake in September of 1968, during my freshman year at Chicago State College, then located at 68$^{th}$ and Stewart Avenue on the South Side. I'm occasionally reminded that she first eyed me during freshman registration. She was beginning her sophomore year and was asked to work the registration desk. I don't recall seeing her, but she laughs when describing what I was wearing–a short sleeve white and lime green double knit shirt, matching green silk and wool dress pants, and dark green slip-on shoes. *"You were this clean, short dude who stood out from the rest of the freshmen,"* she said.

At the start of the school year, I discovered that Ira Carol and I were enrolled in the same biology class, taught by a professor who proclaimed that he invented the seedless watermelon. We talked once in a while, and said hello as we passed each other in the long dark corridors of Chicago State.

During the latter part of my first year, I decided to major in art education. This was prompted by me winning a couple of art contests during my elementary and high school days. To my surprise, Ira Carol was already enrolled in the art program, having majored in commercial art at Dunbar High School.

We were classmates and became friends. This blossoming friendship led to artistic collaborations on art projects we worked on. During this time, I noticed that she and another male art student seemed to have a closer relationship than she and I.

*Dad and the boys. Early 1980.*

After much internal agony, I mustered up enough courage to ask her, "Do you have a boyfriend?" She responded, "*I go out with Mack every now and then.*" I was hoping she would say no, but her answer didn't bother me much. There were a couple of other girls at school, Janet and Patricia, who I sometimes hung out with as well.

One day on the way home after school, I boarded an eastbound Chicago Transit Authority bus on 69th Street. After dropping my coins into the collection box, I stumbled toward the rear of the swaying bus. To my surprise, there she was. I flopped down next to her. As we made gentle contact with our shoulders, our knees were touching through the old faded blue jeans worn by most art majors.

She and I nervously talked about school until I made my move. "I live on 88th and Langley. Why don't you come by sometime," I murmured. She looked me in the eyes with a mischievous smile on her face and responded, "*I'll think about it.*" "I'll cook you a steak dinner," I said without thinking. I don't know where that promise came from.

To my surprise, about two weeks later, she agreed to visit me. It took another three weeks for me to build up enough courage to tell her that I was still living at home with my mother. Ira Carol did visit me, although I don't think I ever cooked that steak dinner for her.

# D

*I have seen you before but this was different*
*We talked and as I gazed into your eyes*
*All sense of time faded away*
*I got lost in the moment*
*The ecstasy of this time*
*And then we touched*
*I can't recall when it happened*
*But our lips met*
*My knees buckled*
*All things around us faded*
*Only the sustained kiss prevailed*
*That moment…your touch*
*Justification for all that we have shared since*
*The gentle kiss, the caressing touch*
*Your bedroom eyes*
*An unforgettable moment*
*Which blended into years of happiness*
*In a fruitful and loving marriage*
*Ira Carol*

While studying at Chicago State, Ira Carol spent many hours in the audio room listening to classical music through headphones. This activity was part of our Music Appreciation class, which was required for graduation. The headphones probably saved her from the peer pressure she would have endured if her friends knew she was listening to classical music back in 1969. I did not like this class.

Thanks to Ira Carol, classical music was always a part of our home environment, and was played constantly, along with the Temptations, OJays, Marvin Gaye, and other rhythm and blues favorites. I even grew to appreciate Mozart, Stravinsky, and Sibelius.

Throughout the late 60s and early 70s, my brothers and I and our girlfriends, would meet at my mother's house.

We played games and spent hours playing bongo drums and wooden flutes purchased at the nearby African shop located at 86th and Cottage Grove Avenue. This little store was loaded with all types of items that looked to be from Africa, but were probably made in China or Japan. There were many different drums, wooden flutes, scarves, dashikis and other clothing items, hand marimbas, and African sculptures of various sizes. When we had our rendezvous, the girls would sing as the boys improvised on the drums and wooden flutes. We had some great times in a small converted bedroom in MuDear's house. This little square room had a black vinyl sofa, matching black beanbag, a small cocktail table, and a small television set with the famous "rabbit ear" antennas, which were tipped with squeezed aluminum foil to enhance reception. This room was called the half a family room because it was so small. Even though MuDear was always close by, we had some great fun here. Well, she sometimes drove down to Memphis without us. This was when the good times really started rolling. My brothers and I gave some great parties when MuDear went on her trips.

This was a time when the black community was fighting for its civil rights. Many African American teenagers and adults who were "caught up" in the *Black Power* movement, used the chant, "Ungawa, Black Power," as an affectionate greeting. I used it many times *back in the day*.

DEMARRE MCGILL

*Rabbit ear antennas and old 45 rpm records. McGill family photo.*

During this time, countless males and females wore huge Afro hairstyles, and large colorful dashikis. Ira Carol hand stitched one for me. She chose a beautiful turquoise blue fabric with intricate orange, blue, and magenta African print designs. Ira Carol worked tirelessly sewing this beautiful garment. I wore this dashiki for years, until it became too small for my bulging frame. I laugh when I look at some of the old photographs taken during this rebellious time.

My Afro hairstyle was big and my beard was long. Some of my friends said that I looked like a Black Manchurian Warrior because I frequently stated that I would not get a haircut or shave until the Vietnam War ended. I still have an old driver's license photo from this period, and it scares me when I look at it.

We spent many days and nights at the Point, a large grassy area forming a u-shaped extension into Lake Michigan at 56th Street. We walked the stone shoreline, tossing rocks, talking, and occasionally stopping to hug and kiss. Some of the people who frequently visited the Point stated that the United States Military maintained an underground missile silo here, but this did not bother us.

Another fantastic area just south of the Point at 63rd Street, motivated the music making we were attempting in MuDear's house. This area contained park benches, a large asphalt parking lot, and was directly adjacent to a large grey stone park beach house. Some of the city's best Conga and Bongo drummers, flutist, and other instrumentalists, met here practically every evening during the summer months and made some of the most inspiring Afrocentric music that could be found outside of the *Mother Country*. These amateur musicians and professionals attracted hundreds of people, from senior citizens, to babies in strollers, or on the backs of fathers, mothers, brothers, or sisters.

Many individuals and families came from far away to witness this cultural extravaganza. The rhythmic thunder of the loud drums, and the sweet sounds of the instrumentalists made the stiffest non-dancers move to the driving beats, including me. If people just happened to walk by carrying drums, or other instruments, all they had to do was find a spot and start playing. No training or audition was needed, although all the musicians had to be able to keep a beat. The spontaneity of this music making was incredible. Some of the spectators would be so moved by the sounds; they would enter the circle forming the musicians and dance until exhausted, or until another dancer forced them out.

*South Side lake front musicians. McGill family photo.*

Marijuana use and the drinking of cheap wines were popular during this time. Boones Farm-Strawberry Hill, Ripple, and the most toxic one, Wild Irish Rose, were popular back then. I am not sure if they could truthfully be called wines. It's questionable whether they contained any natural plant ingredients. The musicians and spectators were, "feeling their oats," as Mama used to say. I sure was feeling mine!

The crowd showed its satisfaction to the musicians and dancers with loud cheers and hand clapping. Ira Carol, being one of the original dancers with the late Joseph Holmes African Dance Troop in Chicago, would start dancing wherever she was. It didn't matter, this lady had to express herself. She would feel the music and would definitely show it. I wish I had recorded more of these musical memories, for they were truly wonderful. Ira Carol and I spent many hours on the lakefront and everyone had fun here.

Anthony was just like his mother. When he was four or five years old, he loved to dance. Play any music and he expressed himself through movement. Ira Carol was always active in teaching and taking dance classes. She frequently took Anthony with her. I'm sure this motivated and influenced his dancing. Anthony and his mother haven't changed much since his younger days, they still love to dance. He has never been unwilling to dance with his mother. On many occasions, when I was not in the mood for dancing, Anthony would grab his mother's hand and lead her to the dance floor.

## *DANCE BETWEEN TWO MOONS*

*Oh! Great Darkness*
*Absent of light*
*I dance with joy*
*This very night*
*Captured in the moment*
*Exuberant and free*
*I give to the dance*
*The totality of me*
*Ira Carol*
*1-7-92*

The Black Panther Party was strong and active in Chicago and the West coast during the time we were dating. This organization was threatening to some, but many people in African American communities throughout Chicago looked upon the Black Panther Party as a positive organization that was focused on self-determination, self-protection, and feeding neighborhood children.

During the mid to late 60s, the local chapter of the Black Panthers focused their feeding program on the West Side of Chicago. These activities were slowed considerably when in 1969, the Illinois States Attorney's Office, under the leadership of Edward Hanrahan and the FBI, shot their way into the West Side apartment of Mark Clark and Fred Hampton.

The officers used information provided to them by a Black Panther informant to pinpoint where members were sleeping. Clark and Hampton were the leaders of the Chicago Chapter of the Black Panther Party. The investigation of this incident discovered that the FBI and Chicago police officers fired over ninety bullets into the building and the apartment where Mark Clark and Fred Hampton were sleeping, and one other bullet "possibly" came from a Black Panther member. Both men died in this onslaught, which many people around the country labeled a government political assassination.

The States Attorney's Office justified the killings by stating that upon entering the building to conduct a search warrant, many shots were fired at them by the Black Panther members. Extensive investigations following this incident revealed conclusively that all but one of the shots fired into this building were from the guns of the on scene police officers and FBI.

The friendship between Ira Carol and I grew like Mr. Avery Fisher's, "flowers that must bloom at a particular time." We dated until our marriage in 1973.

Ira Carol was apprehensive about having children. She could not imagine herself being pregnant. We eventually started to talk about raising a family and decided to have two children. We both did not want to have an only child, and hoped to eventually have a boy and a girl. On August 28, 1975, two years after we were married, our first child, Demarre Lavelle McGill was born. I didn't want him to be named Jr., so we gave him a middle name.

My brother, who is two years younger than me, is named James McGill Jr. Family and friends called him Junior until he was well into his thirties. I didn't want this for my son.

# *STEPS*

*Me a mother? I couldn't imagine or even conceive of the idea of being a mother. I used every possible excuse I could think of; too young, not ready, unprepared. At age twenty-six and married for two years, giving birth to a child was a major step that I was not sure I wanted to take.*

*Growing up as the oldest of six children, and my experiences while teaching in the Chicago Public School System had been an eye opener for me. What sort of parent would I be? I could not answer this question, but I was definite about one thing, under no circumstance would I allow a child of mine to run my household.*

*I realized that it was very important for me to find out what my husband's view of parenting was. I had to mentally process this unfamiliar topic. I soon realized that this had to be a step-by-step process.*

*The first step was a visit to my gynecologist. I sat in his office, watching all the expectant mothers walk by. Step two happened when I started reading mother-to-be books. I started drawing and painting pregnant women during step three. The fourth step was on a much more personal level, crying and praying about childbirth while massaging my abdomen. The final step was my complete acceptance and excitement about being pregnant and becoming a mother. Ira Carol*

Ira Carol's first pregnancy was a beautiful, but traumatic experience for both of us, especially my wife. We attended Lamaze classes at Michael Reese Hospital, where the instructors taught the expectant mothers and fathers relaxation and breathing techniques designed to ease the emotional trauma and pain of childbirth.

The most exciting times during the pregnancy were when we sat down to eat. Every time Ira Carol fed herself, Demarre started moving around inside her. Demarre loved to eat then, and he definitely has not changed much, he still loves to eat. We felt a joyful but strange sensation when our open hands were placed on Ira Carol's abdomen and we felt Demarre moving. He knew it was feeding time and was showing his happiness. The movement also told us that he was still living.

# DEMARRE MCGILL

*I am thankful for the food that I eat*
*It might taste really bad,*
*But makes me really sad,*
*When I think of what some children don't have,*
*I am very fortunate for as much as I eat,*
*So I never waste the food that I munch with my teeth.*
*Demarre Lavelle McGill*
*1985, 10-years-old*

Just as she did during her college days, Ira Carol enjoyed listening to classical music during her pregnancies. On many occasions she placed her abdomen close to our big Fisher stereo speakers so that her babies could hear this music. At the time, I didn't think unborn babies could hear, but I didn't let her know how I felt. Many other people didn't believe this either.

During a visit to the famous Tanglewood Music Center to hear Demarre perform with the Fellowship Orchestra, a man approached us and asked, "How did you all produce such musically talented children?" Ira Carol mentioned some of the McGill's Principles we used, including finding the best teachers. She also said, "*I placed my abdomen close to our speakers so that Demarre and Anthony could hear the music I was playing.*" The person who asked this question seemed shocked by my wife's answer. Demarre also seemed surprised. After the person walked away he said, "Mama, don't mention that again. People might think you're strange for saying that." Many researchers including neuroscientists have proven that unborn babies hear and respond to music and other sounds.

In an article by William J. Cromie, entitled, *Music on the Brain,* he wrote:

Babies come into the world with musical preferences. They begin to respond to music while still in the womb. At age 4 months, dissonant notes at the end of a melody will cause them to squirm and turn away. If they like a tune, they may coo. *(Harvard University Gazette, March 22, 2001)*

Although it is a proven fact that an unborn infant can hear, it is unknown whether this improves their intelligence after birth, or makes them better musicians. This means nothing to my wife. She still believes that her health conscious diet during her pregnancies, her attempt to be stress free, playing classical music for her unborn children, and the McGill's Principles, all helped to make her sons successful classical musicians.

At about 11:00 P.M. on a late August night, Ira Carol woke me and screamed; *"I think the baby is coming. The baby is coming."* We jumped out of bed, dressed, and rushed to the hospital about six miles away. My mind was racing as fast as my car. My inner voice was asking, "What if the baby came while we were in the car?" "What will I do?" I was a nervous wreck and I'm lucky I didn't crash our car.

We used the Lamaze breathing techniques while driving to the hospital. The drive seemed to take a few hours instead of fifteen minutes. We also did Lamaze breathing during her long labor ordeal.

When we arrived at the hospital, Ira Carol was quickly transported to the maternity ward. The doctor examined her. Although she felt pain, she had not dilated. The following day, Dr. Meltzer, her personal physician arrived. The doctor caused pain during his examination and Ira Carol hit him on the arm and screamed, *"Stop."* She was in labor so long, the custodian from the previous day came in and said, "You're still here?" Ira's pain tolerance during this time was low. I held her hand and we did Lamaze breathing for hours on end. It did not seem to work. When my wife reminisces about this experience, she talks about the feeling of the bones in her pelvic area separating. *"Twice in my life I have felt my skeletal system move…it was not a good feeling."* What really freaked her out was the fear of knowing that after many hours of painful labor, there was no turning back. *"At that point, I truly knew there was a God, and I really needed his help."*

She requested that the doctor perform a Cesarean section procedure to relieve the pain and to, *"Get it over with."* Dr. Meltzer reassured us that this procedure was not needed and refused to do it.

Finally, at 11:02 A.M., Demarre Lavelle McGill was born. He was a healthy seven pound three ounce baby. We thought something was wrong with him because his skull was so elongated. All the doctors and nurses said, "This is normal." The next day his head seemed to have reshaped itself. The elongated shape had miraculously disappeared. He looked beautiful. This was the start of many happy days and nights for our family.

One of the most difficult decisions we had to make was whether Ira Carol should breast-feed Demarre. We both toiled with this question and made the decision not to breast-feed. Ira Carol felt guilty, but ultimately got over it. She did hold Demarre's head close to her breast during bottle-feeding sessions. She felt this closeness was important for our new baby. She was right.

After giving birth, the glow on my wife's face was like that of a full moon on a beautiful summer night. When she thinks or talks about her sons, that radiant smile returns.

The joy of knowing that our sons are living productive lives, and influencing people through their music is hard to describe. They are making a living doing something they love to do, touching people's lives by making beautiful music.

## *MUSIC FLOWS*

*Music flows through my son's like the fluid that gives an infant life*
*Like the fuel that keeps an airplane in flight*
*The heartbeat of sound rings within their veins*

*The very fiber of their being is echoed with every note vibrating through*
*their brains*
*Music flows...Music of the mind, music of endless time*
*Enter unto me as the stars are to the universe*
*Music flows...stay and pulsate with the rhythmic sensation of thirst*
*Merge my thoughts only of you as my soul would want me to*
*Oh music! I seek you in my dreams*
*Oh music! Without you I would scream*
*Music flows...Music of the mind*
*Music flows...Music without time!*
*Music Flows*
*Ira Carol, 2-19-92*

Ira Carol was thinking of her tremendously talented and suc-cessful sons when she wrote *Music Flows.*

Dr. Meltzer also delivered our second child, Anthony Barrone McGill. His middle name is in honor of Barrone, who died in a car crash in 1979. Roni was responsible for me becoming a Chicago firefighter. He constantly asked if I was going to take the firefighters exam, which was administered by the City of Chicago in 1978. "Are you taking the test?" he asked me so many times I finally told him "Yes." I took the exam and was hired in 1980.

Ira Carol was only in labor for about four hours, and had a much easier and less painful pregnancy with Anthony. She was physically active while carrying him. My wife smiles when she talks about the feeling she got when Anthony kicked her as she rolled on the floor to demonstrate a movement to her students while teaching an elementary school dance class. Anthony didn't move as much as his brother. This caused her to sit up and cry because of a fear that Anthony was not healthy. Every now and then, Anthony kicked his mother to let her know that he was all right.

Ira Carol cried a lot while carrying Anthony. She kept a clean supply of Kleenex facial tissue in her purse and on the table next to our bed. Because of constant heartburn, she didn't enjoy eating as much, and did not like having to get out of bed and go to work.

When Ira Carol thought she was about to deliver, we again rushed to Michael Reese Hospital. She said, *"We need to get to the hospital"*. My mind flashed back four years earlier when Demarre was about to be born. The large number of pregnant women in the maternity ward was beyond belief. They were everywhere, in the rooms, the hallway, and my wife was placed on a bed in a storage room. Was this legal? I don't know, and frankly, at this point in time I didn't care.

*When I was in my last term of pregnancy, I sat Demarre down and had a talk with him about my having another baby. Before I talked to him about this subject, and to make my job easier, I purchased the book 'Where Did I Come From' written by Peter Mayle. After talking and reading the book to him, Demarre wanted me to show him where the baby came out. I told him that this happens in the hospital. I wasn't about to get that descriptive, but I did spend some time explaining the process to him. I tried not to be shocked about the questions that he asked me. He even asked his daddy one of those eyebrow-lifting questions. We had taken him to an amusement park, and his daddy took him into the public restroom, which had no doors. As I was standing outside waiting for them to come out, I heard Demarre ask his daddy, 'Does mama have a penis.' Now it was my husband's time to have one of those talks with Demarre. Ira Carol*

It is normal for children to ask questions. Sometimes parents may have to visit a library or bookstore to find the best way to answer them. In today's technological world, the Internet can also be used. The main thing to remember here is that a child's mind is always working overtime, and as parents, don't shrug off or ignore their questions. Find a way to answer all of them.

Anthony was born at 8:44 PM on July 17, 1979. He was a beautiful seven pound four ounce baby. I was able to build up enough courage to watch the entire birth a few feet from the delivery bed.

When I think about the time Ira Carol was in the maternity ward giving birth to Demarre, I wish I had also been there to witness his birth. To see Anthony being born was not a pretty sight, but it was a beautiful experience. Every father should witness this miracle first hand. To actually see the top of Anthony's head exposed within my wife's womb was unreal. During the next few minutes, with the help of Dr. Meltzer and the nurses, Anthony wiggled out. I swear I saw a toy clarinet in his right hand.

The umbilical cord was cut. The nurses wiped him off with large white towels, wrapped him in another big towel, and handed him to my wife. We looked at each other, smiled, and stared at Anthony Barrone McGill. Ira Carol seemed to be in a trance, but her quiet smile calmed my throbbing heart. She handed Anthony to me and I held him in my arms. My smile turned into an all teeth showing grin, but my mind was racing trying to understand this miracle of life.

Demarre and Anthony were born four years apart. We planned it this way. We felt that a child should have the opportunity to enjoy his parents and be spoiled. I use this word affectionately. We did not allow them to do whatever they wanted, and knew that we had to set rules, limits, and establish guidelines, and enforce them with firmness and consistency.

*My husband and I were affectionate towards our children, and made sure that they would not divide us when it came to granting or not granting their request for something. If Demarre or Anthony asked me for something and I said no, I knew they would go to their father and make the same request. My husband would always check with me to see if they had asked me first. We called this 'checks and balances.'*

*As clever as children are, there were times when they managed to get around this. When we found out they had successfully maneuvered around these 'checks and balances,' we didn't get too upset. We sat them down and talked to them and did not blow these situations out of proportion. Ira Carol*

After consulting with a friend who was a registered Naprapath, Ira Carol became even more health conscious when Demarre and Anthony were children. She began preparing meals that included more fruits, vegetables, nuts, and less red meat. A short time later, her healthy eating plan rubbed off on us. After a few months of no pork or beef, we all became accustomed to the new change in diet. I missed my pork chops the most, but soon got used to more poultry and fish. We also attempted to limit the amount of sugar and salt we consumed on a daily basis. We didn't become strict vegetarians, and allowed Demarre and Anthony to have a burger or two if they wanted, or a large order of McDonald's fries.

Today, Ira Carol and I continue to follow this diet plan, which I think has prevented us from having any serious health problems. To this day, Demarre and Anthony are conscious about the foods and drinks they consume.

When I reminisce about these early days of our young family, I say to myself, "Where did the time go?" It seems like yesterday that Ira Carol and I were painting with oil on canvas, sculpting red clay busts in our art classes at Chicago State College, playing catch, or kicking soccer balls with our sons on the shore of Lake Michigan.

Parents, realize that the time you have with your children is fleeting. You have them for a very short time. Cherish these few years as you raise them to be positive and successful men and women.

The joy you will experience when daydreaming about these times will bring a smile to your face, and on many occasions, you will cry while thinking about the good and the trying times you shared with your children. Use every possible second, minute, hour, and day to teach them. Love, motivate, and guide your sons and daughters so they may someday thank you for, "raising them well."

*Ira Carol and Demarre, one month before Anthony's birth.*

*Demarre, Anthony, and me in front of Dr. Martin Luther King's birth home in Atlanta, Georgia.*

# CHAPTER SIX

## CHICAGO'S SOUTH SIDE AND THE AUGUST 28 QUADRANT

Demarre Lavelle and Anthony Barrone McGill were born and raised in the Chatham and the West Chesterfield neighborhoods located on the South Side of Chicago, places where some African American boys and girls never get to see adulthood. Demarre and Anthony, however, are now professional classical musicians in a field where few African Americans exist.

For some people, when the South Side of Chicago is mentioned, visions of Al Capone, or organized street gangs come to mind.

Before Anthony's solo performance of the Mozart Clarinet Concerto with the Birmingham, Alabama Symphony Orchestra on October 10, 2010, Mr. Michael Huebner, of the *Birmingham News* wrote:

> Chicago's South Side often gets a bad rap. At times portrayed as a crime-ridden area of decaying housing, rough neighborhoods and street gangs, it was spotlighted in the 1994 documentary, *Hoop Dreams,* which chronicled two teenager's hopes of escaping the 'projects' through basketball.
>
> Although violent crime persists area wide, a broader view reveals an ethnically diverse region with some of the world's finest architectural landmarks and cultural and educational institutions, and a reputation as a Mecca for gospel and rhythm and blues.

Chicago's South Side does indeed "get a bad rap." The film, *Hoop Dreams* is not a microcosm of the entire South Side. Although drugs, gangs, crime, and the violence these bring to many communities exist, the entire South Side is not the cesspool of drugs and crime that media depictions sensationalize in the name of *news.*

These tales of South Side blues hides from public view the many stories of those who live productive lives and those who transcend the negative stereotypes. In truth, the vast majority of Chicago's South Side residents are ordinary, hard-working citizens trying to provide the best for their families. There are many South Side neighborhoods with well-kept homes and manicured lawns on beautiful tree lined streets.

Now, as well as throughout Chicago's illustrious history, many of this country's most successful and well-known African American business, political, cultural, educational, and religious leaders called the South Side home. President Barack Obama lived much of his adult life on the South Side. Demarre and Anthony are part of this long history, as they were also born and raised on the South Side of Chicago.

Ira Carol and I are proud to say that we still reside here, in a home and neighborhood we have lived in for over thirty-five years. As young parents, the task of raising two successful African American males was our number one goal.

My wife and I decided during the early years of our marriage, if we had any children, they would be raised in a nurturing and supportive household. Our primary goal was to ensure that our children had everything they needed to become triumphant in life. This does not mean that we gave Demarre and Anthony everything they asked for. There were many times when we told them "no."

Ira Carol and I can honestly say that as a result of the love, support, encouragement, and the guidance we provided, Demarre and Anthony grew up to be successful African American men who are positively influencing people's lives through their actions and their music. The success they achieved was not, "written in stone," it was a family and extended "family affair."

Throughout our lives, we have heard people use the words, "pay now or pay later." I have no idea who first used this phrase, but it is one Ira Carol and I adopted after our children were born. By this we meant that we would spend the last penny in our possession, and use every resource available to raise our children. It was not easy, but we accomplished our child-raising goals without having to *pay later.*

My wife and I are not exceptions to the rule when it comes to raising children. There are millions of untold stories of families across the world that raised successful men and women.

One of the greatest moments of my life was August 28, 1975, the day Demarre was born. The memory of that day will be with me forever. When Demarre was six-years-old, Billy Saulsberry, a family friend, picked him up and asked, "What do you want to be when you grow up?" Demarre quickly, responded by saying, "I want to be a man when I grow up." Everyone in the room heard Demarre's answer and responded positively to the comment.

When he was seven-years-old, he was jumping rope in the back yard of our two flat, four apartment building on 80th and Prairie Street on the South Side of Chicago. Michael, one of my high school classmates who rented one of the apartments from my mother and me, entered the backyard and saw Demarre with an old cracked vinyl clothesline in his hand. Michael immediately looked at Demarre and asked him, "What are you doing, jumping rope? That's a girl's game." Without hesitation, Demarre responded:

"Muhammad Ali jumps ropes."

Michael realized that he had been out-smarted by a seven-year-old, turned and slowly walked the two flights up the old wooden exterior stairs to his second floor apartment. The message here is, no matter what age, children's minds are working overtime, and they will often out think the smartest adult.

Do not underestimate what their minds are capable of. As adults, we often think of our young children as non-thinkers. Don't be fooled by this illusion. They are thinking while we are awake and when we are asleep. Sometimes while we are teaching them, they are teaching us. This is an amazing and wonderful concept that adults should realize is possible, and happens more often than you might think. You also have to be there to experience these fascinating conversations and exchanges, and mentally and digitally record these early interactions between your child and other adults. Be there with and for your child. You might learn something about him and yourself.

I'm happy to report that thirty years later, Demarre is in fact a man, and is a graduate of Curtis Institute of Music in Philadelphia, and in 1998 received his Master of Music degree from the Juilliard School in New York. These are among the premier music schools in the world.

Demarre has performed solo with orchestras throughout the United States. The following are some of these ensembles: the Seattle Symphony, San Diego Symphony, the Chicago Symphony, Philadelphia Orchestra, Pittsburgh Symphony, Baltimore Symphony, Toledo Symphony, Dayton Philharmonic, Milwaukee Symphony, Hilton Head Symphony Orchestra, Oberlin Chamber Orchestra, Florida Orchestra, and the Juilliard Symphony. He has also performed in France, Germany, Austria, Hungary, Japan, South Korea, St. Barts and South Africa.

Although Demarre has worked extremely hard all of his young life, and has achieved many of his goals, his music career is not filled with all success stories. He was unsuccessful in flute auditions for jobs in several major orchestras in the United States, including the Chicago Symphony, located in the city of his birth. Although he was hurt emotionally after initially not being successful in his attempts to secure a seat in a professional orchestra, he was determined to not give up his quest.

Ira Carol and I always told our sons to always think positively, even after experiencing setbacks. Our constant mantra was, "Think positive, no matter what." Each time he auditioned, we truly expected him to win the position and he expected it also.

On several occasions when he was in his early twenties, Ira Carol and I cried after he called to tell us that he was not successful in the audition. We did not let Demarre know that our tears were flowing, but we knew how hard he had worked to prepare himself and we could not control our emotions. We consoled ourselves by saying, "His time will come." "Never give up," was another of my wife's mottos and one she constantly drilled into our sons' minds. In fact, I did the same thing, only my motto was *think positive.* "Positive Thinking Creates a Strong Mind and Body," were the words on a large sign hanging in my classrooms during my eight year teaching career in the public school system of Chicago. A similar sign could also be found in our home.

Demarre knows how difficult it is to win a position in an orchestra. He understands the internal and external politics that come into play during professional symphony orchestra auditions. Demarre says that he understands the process and this has helped him retrace his steps back to 1991, when at age fifteen he said: "I don't want to be famous, I want to be the best."

The personal satisfaction he gets from practicing constantly to reach his goals has had a calming affect on him. During our family's 2001 Thanksgiving dinner in Chicago, Demarre mentioned that he recently watched the videotape of his 1991 Illinois Young Performers solo concerto with the Chicago Symphony Orchestra.

This connection to the past reconfirmed his ultimate goal of being the best flutist he could possibly be. He recently stated that no matter where he ends up, his quest to be the best would not end there, and would continue throughout his life.

He also said if he remains with the great Dallas Symphony Orchestra, he will continue to do all he can to make this orchestra, "the best in the world." Before joining the Dallas Symphony, Demarre won the Seattle Symphony Orchestra principal flute position in the spring of 2011. Before this appointment, he was the principal flutist with the San Diego Symphony Orchestra, the Florida Orchestra, and the Santa Fe Opera Orchestra. Making beautiful music is his lifelong passion that he uses to make peoples' lives better.

In January of 2010, Demarre was chosen by the *San Diego Magazine* as one of "50 People to Watch in 2010." The magazine described the honorees as, "an eclectic mix of San Diegans worth watching in the new year…get to know some personalities on the rise."

In honor of Black History Month, on February 12, 2010, Demarre was selected by the readers of the *San Diego News Network* and local politicians as one of "Eight Great Young Black San Diego Community Leaders." Through his music and leadership, Demarre is enriching the lives of people across this country and the world.

August 28 is significant to us for three other reasons. Dr. Martin Luther King, Jr. delivered his *I have a Dream* speech on August 28, 1963, on the steps of the Lincoln Memorial in Washington D. C. The 250,000 people who participated in the "March on Washington," witnessed this historic speech.

On August 28, 2008, candidate Barack Obama delivered his acceptance speech after being nominated to be the Democratic Party's candidate to run against Senator John McCain for the Presidency of the United States of America. Illinois Senator Obama became the first African American in the history of this country to be nominated by a major political party to run for the presidency. The world knows that on November 4, 2008, Senator Barack Obama was elected overwhelmingly to be the President of the United States of America, and took office on January 20, 2009. President Obama's three hundred sixty-five electoral votes were one hundred ninety-two more than Senator John McCain's total. The sixty-nine million people who voted for Senator Obama had accomplished a feat that many Americans thought to be impossible.

In retrospect, Dr. Martin Luther King, Jr. envisioned this historical moment. On April 3, 1968, Dr. King delivered one of his most famous speeches at the Mason Temple (Church of God In Christ headquarters) in Memphis, Tennessee. Dr. King travelled to Memphis to support the city's sanitation workers who were on strike at the time.

The following is a quote from the speech Dr. King delivered the day before he was assassinated:

I have been to the mountaintop. Well, I don't know what will happen now. We've got some difficult days ahead. But it really doesn't matter with me now, because I've been to the mountaintop. I just want to do God's will. And He's allowed me to go up to the mountain.

And I've looked over. And I've seen the Promised Land. I may not get there with you. But I want you to know tonight, that we, as a people, will get to the Promised Land!

*Dr. Martin Luther King, Jr. Memorial in Washington D. C. Photo by D. McGill.*

I am not sure if African Americans have reached Dr. King's "Promised Land" yet, but the election of Barack Obama surely brought us one step closer to the land Dr. King talked about. Dr. King was a visionary and understood that through hard work, dedication, and sacrifice, African Americans would someday accomplish things few people in this country or the world could have ever imagined.

During an interview with Bob McKenzie of BBC in 1964, four years before his famous, *I Have Been To The Mountaintop* speech,

Dr. King predicted that the United States would elect an African American President within twenty-five years. McKenzie mentioned that when Robert Kennedy was U. S. Attorney General (1961-1964), he predicted that within forty years, this country would have an African American President. Dr. King was more optimistic and responded with the following statement:

> Well, let me say first that I think it is necessary to make it clear that there are Negroes who are presently qualified to be President of the United States. There are many who are qualified in terms of integrity, in terms of vision, in terms of leadership ability. But we do know there are certain problems, and prejudices, and morays in our society, which make it difficult.
>
> Now however, I am very optimistic about the future. Frankly, I have seen changes in the United States over the last two years that surprised me. I've seen levels of compliance with the Civil Rights Bill and changes that have been most surprising. So, on the basis of this, I think we may be able to get a Negro President in less than forty years. I would think that this could come in twenty-five years or less. *(BBC World News America, January 20, 2009)*

Dr. Martin Luther King, Jr. and Attorney General Robert Kennedy did not live to witness the election of the first African American President—assassins' bullets killed them in 1968. These leaders were positive thinkers whose vision became a reality in our lifetime.

Dr. King and Robert Kennedy set very high goals for themselves, and for the African American community. As parents, you must set high goals for your lives and the lives of your children. We know that President Barack Obama set one of the highest goals any African American could possibly set for himself. After seeing and hearing

Senator Obama deliver the keynote speech during the Democratic National Convention on July 27, 2004, I was not surprised when he won the Presidency of the United States. While watching the speech, I said, "This man could someday be President."

The final link of the August 28 quadrant is not pretty. It is tragic. On August 28, 1955, Emmett Till, a fifteen-year-old African American boy from Chicago's South Side was brutally murdered in Money, Mississippi.

Emmett Till's death brought much needed international attention to the plight of African Americans across this nation, who suffered brutal physical and mental abuses during this "Jim Crow" era.

Demarre was born twenty years to the day after two white men in Mississippi murdered Emmitt Till. As I look back on the time when Demarre and Anthony were fifteen-years-old, I understood then and now, why it is so important for parents to raise their children, to be there with them through the ups and downs of their early years.

Since 1955, civil rights conditions have improved for many, but parents in some communities still wonder if their child will return home alive after leaving for school, or after leaving home for any reason. In many communities throughout the United States, a child does not have to leave home to become a victim of senseless violence. They can simply be sitting on their front porch, or reading a book in their living room.

Too many young African Americans are being murdered in the black community today, not by whites, but by other young African Americans with high-powered semi-automatic weapons. Some say that the level of violence in the black community is at an epidemic level. One can also say that violence in general–among all the people in this country–is out of control. It's going to take all governmental bodies and communities across this nation to rise up and fight the perpetrators of this senseless violence.

No matter how positive our household was, there was no guarantee Demarre and Anthony would survive on Chicago's South Side and become successful adults. The violence that persists on the mean Chicago streets is frightening, and is destroying the lives of our children.

As parents, Ira Carol and I were determined to teach, guide, and protect our sons. We were fortunate they were able to escape the violence and other negative situations found on Chicago's South Side, and become positive contributors to society.

Every day is a challenge when raising children in contemporary urban times. Because of the violence that seems to be spreading across American cities, and bad economic conditions, these challenges may seem difficult to overcome. Parents, meet these challenges head on and do whatever is necessary to overcome them. You will enjoy the "fruits of your labor," as you watch your sons and daughters grow up to be strong men and women.

Anything is possible in this world. Your child can be a teacher, scientist, astronaut, professional athlete, musician, biologist, gymnast, firefighter, and the President of the United States, even if he grew up on the South Side of Chicago.

One thing is obvious; children can't accomplish anything by themselves. They need the nurturing and support provided by loving parents, other family members, and friends. Be there with your children and start to teach and motivate them during the early days and years of their lives, and protect them from life's hazards.

*Demarre and me in 1975.*

# CHAPTER SEVEN

## CREAM WILL ALWAYS RISE TO THE TOP

"Cream always rises," is an old saying that has been around for many years. A family friend once used this quote to lift our spirits after Demarre didn't win a classical music competition when he was a teenager. Many of the other parents in attendance also felt that Demarre had been the best performer, and should have been declared the winner.

Cream, which is considered the richest part of milk based upon the density, smoothness, and taste, will rise to the top when the milk is placed in an open container. This cream can be used to make butter, which is consumed on a daily basis by millions of people around the world.

Ira Carol and I are proud to say Demarre and Anthony are like that cream, which will always rise. As parents, we understood that in order for them to rise to the top and be positive and successful men, we had to provide for their basic needs, and give them unwavering support, every day during the early years of their lives. We understood the importance of loving our children. We understood the importance of providing a positive home environment for them. We understood the importance of disciplining Demarre and Anthony, but our disciplinary actions did not mean physical or mental abuse. We also understood the importance of, "raising them well."

How much emphasis do parents place on raising their children? Do modern day parents allow their children to raise themselves? *American Heritage Dictionary* defines a parent as, "one who begets, gives birth to, or nurtures and raises a child." To raise means to bring up, to teach, to bring to the point of adulthood. The word raise as it relates to children can also mean to provide for all the physical and mental needs of a child until he or she becomes a young adult.

Many parents rely on manuals and books found in bookstores and libraries to find the answers to these and other complex questions associated with raising children. Some parents also seek the guidance of television experts, who seem to have all the answers. These guides and so-called professionals cannot by themselves elevate children to the state of being successful and positive men and women. For parents who are searching for clues, ideas, or suggestions about raising their children, these guides may offer some help, but they do not contain all the answers to the many difficult and complex issues and problems all parents and children face.

Parents must utilize a mind building and hands on approach when raising their children. By this, I mean parents should understand that children's minds, no matter how young and small, are capable of learning. Start to teach them before and after they are born. For example, read and play music for your unborn children. Furthermore, don't wait for the babysitter, or teacher to provide positive influences for them. Spend as many hours of the day as possible with your sons and daughters during these early years. As a parent, your primary job should be to provide everything necessary for your children to be successful.

Some of today's children are nurtured and raised not by parents or other adults, but grow up with artificial parents disguised as television sets, video games, and the many negative sites on the ever-popular Internet. It is obvious that television programs and sites on the Internet are not all negative, but parents or whomever the child is living with must monitor their use.

The positive aspects of parents being with their children, as many minutes and hours as possible during the early years of their lives, cannot be overstated.

If a parent is with his child, chances are good there will be conversation and communication taking place. Even if there is no verbal communication occurring between parent and child, the peace of mind of knowing that your child is in a safe home environment, filled with educational books and toys, is very rewarding.

Seize every opportunity to teach and to instill positive images and messages into your child's mind. We are all aware that parents are children's most important teachers and should be the teachers who spend the most quality time with them.

Based on the daily schedule of working parents, the time spent with children becomes even more precious and should be viewed as the most important part of the day. This is why the quality of this time when parents interact with their children can counteract and balance the hours spent away from them. By being with your child, you occupy time and space which decreases the amount of time left in the day when he or she can watch television, play the ever more violent video or computer games, or hang out with friends.

Organized and structured activities outside of the home are also important for the overall development of your child. The positive social skills learned during interactions with other children are important, and are vital parts of the developmental processes all children go through. The child's socialization activities with other children will also provide opportunities for parents to observe their child while he interacts with others. This observation can be used to identify possible negative social behaviors, which may be exhibited by him. As a result of this observation, you can develop plans to work with your child to address these issues while he is still young.

Children of all ages need discipline and structure in their lives. By exposing them to structured activities, they learn valuable lessons relative to discipline, commitment, and responsibility. They learn the importance of being on time and how to communicate and interact positively with others. In addition to learning the subject matter, the socializing skills learned in music, gymnastics, tennis, basketball, art, writing, or swimming classes, are crucial to developing a well-balanced child.

Allowing your child to participate in various fun activities also exposes him to possible career choices without you even discussing this subject with him. It's fun to talk about these times twenty-five years later, when your adult child's current profession is directly related to one of the activities he was involved in when he was five, six, seven, eight, or nine-years-old. This is real. It happens all the time. This happened to my sons. Those music lessons when they were five and six helped to mold them into the successful professional musicians they are today. Make it happen to your child by exposing him to as many positive activities as possible. Ensure that your child's school provides positive learning environments and activities outside of the school as well.

Parents, you must find the time to be there with your sons and daughters during these activities. The mental and physical support you provide during these early years is crucial, and is a major part of the process of raising your children.

# DEMARRE MCGILL

Today is the last day of school. We went to the
Nutcracker. We really did enjoy it. After that, we had
a Christmas party. The Christmas party was really fun.
We had candy, chips, juice, and cake.
Anthony Barrone McGill, 8-years-old
Journal Entry 12-18-87

*Instill in your children that they should develop the courage, fortitude,
and determination to be whatever they want to be. As a parent, always help
your children focus on their positive achievements, not the pitfalls that all
children will ultimately face in life. My son Demarre once said to me,* 'I'm
inspired by failure not defeated by it.'

*Help to ensure their success by being aware of, and tapping into your
children's creative energy. As a parent, you may not be a musician, artist,
swimmer, or gymnast, but you can expose your children to these activities
and more by finding the right programs and teachers for them.*

*Parental observation and intuition are important keys in making decisions
about your children. For example, when Demarre was young, he loved to play
his cousin's piano, write short stories, do wheelies on his bike, roller skate, and
play basketball. To support these interests, my husband and I sought out formal
classes where he learned the correct and safe way to do these things.*

*One of the few rules we enforced with Demarre and Anthony was if they
started any classes or activities, they were obligated to complete them. Ira
Carol*

For two summers during their pre-teen years, Demarre and
Anthony spent the day studying Tae Kwon Do with Master Carlos
Lavington at Nat King Cole Park, located a few blocks from our
home. Master Lavington is a short, dark complexion bald headed
man, who was always fit. This strong African American was well
respected by all the children and adults who visited his park to play
basketball, football, baseball, jog, or just picnic under a tree. He
did not allow troublemakers in Cole Park. He was tough, but had a
calming and positive effect on all the children.

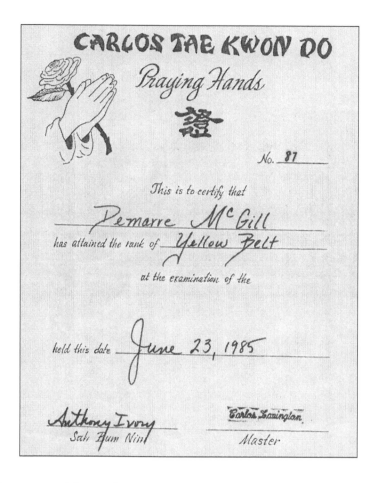

Our sons ultimately rose to the rank of blue belt at Cole Park. They learned self-discipline, self-respect, self-control, and many other important life lessons in the classes. Along with these mental attributes, they also learned the art of self-defense. The twelve dollars per month fee we paid was quite low when compared to the valuable lessons learned under Master Lavington's guidance.

The physical activities of the Tae Kwon Do classes kept their bodies in great shape. They were never overweight. To this day, Demarre and Anthony understand the importance of being both mentally and physically fit, and still work out regularly.

Ira Carol and I always heard people talk about the importance of exposing infants to swimming. My first formal swimming lesson didn't happen until I was in high school and I wiggled out of taking swimming by faking a medical problem. Back in those days, boys at my high school were not allowed to swim in swimming trunks. They had to come to the pool naked. I thought this was weird and couldn't see myself walking around naked among a bunch of thirty-five other boys. The teacher justified this practice by saying that wet swimming trunks would cause the lockers to rust and deteriorate. I still wonder if this was a citywide policy.

We did not want Demarre to be a non-swimmer. When he was seven-months-old, one month before he began to walk, we enrolled him in a swimming class at the 111th Street YMCA, located on the far South Side of Chicago. We were nervous when the swimming instructor put him in the water for the first time and let him go. His survival instincts took over, and he instinctively held his breath and started moving his arms and legs. Within a few seconds he floated to the surface. The seconds seemed like a few long minutes to us. After much apprehension, he soon was able to move in the water and seemed to enjoy the experience. A few years later, he was swimming like a fish and diving off the highest board at Chicago State University, where Anthony also took lessons.

As he got older, we enrolled him in other programs such as gymnastics and tennis. I thought Demarre was going to be a great tennis player. Watching him play tennis caused me to have visions of a young Arthur Ashe being in the family. Demarre and Anthony excelled in all the activities we enrolled them in.

As he was growing up, I taught him some of the things I learned as a child down in Memphis. One was how to create a high pitched whistling sound by placing a broadleaf piece of grass or leaf vertically between the thumbs, and then blowing air between the thumbs. This caused the grass to vibrate, creating a high-pitched sound. Another sound producing technique I taught Demarre was to place his thumbs together in an upward direction and inter-lock his fingers, then close the hands, leaving an air pocket inside the closed hands. Blowing air between the thumbs causes a low-pitched sound to emanate from the locked hands.

Demarre was totally impressed with the fact that he could create various sounds by blowing air into his closed hands. He treated his hands as an instrument long before he took his first music lesson. If Demarre didn't have anything else in his hands, he was making sounds with them. We have an old videotape that was filmed by me during a Sunday school program about thirty-three years ago. Demarre is five-years-old and can be seen making sounds with his hands.

While in elementary school, when Demarre finished his class work, he would make these sounds. One of his teachers could not get him to stop doing this during class and requested that we meet with her. My wife met with the teacher and Demarre at the school, and convinced him that it was not appropriate for him to do this while in class. We recently found another old video of Demarre making sounds with his hands during a class play. I am not sure if the simple act of me sharing these experiences with Demarre helped him to develop musically, but today he is not blowing air into his hands, he is blowing into a professional model flute in front of thousands of people.

Parents should share the simplest things with their children by talking to them. Think about your own personal childhood experiences and choose those, which were fun and had a positive effect on you, or might spur their imagination and creativity.

Ira Carol and I talked to our children. We told many stories about our childhood. We talked about how my brothers and I caught large emerald green or golden brown beetles (we called them June bugs,) tied sewing thread to their legs and flew them like kites. I thought my brothers and I were the only kids in the world who did this until on a cold snowy night in Glencoe, Illinois (February 9, 2010), Ira Carol and I attended a live theater production called

*Old Settler.* A character named Husband played the male role. I nudged Ira Carol's arm when Husband, while discussing his early childhood growing up in the South, also tied thread to the legs of beetles and flew them like kites. This line surprised me. I smiled for the next fifteen minutes, knowing that one of my childhood activities (cruelty to insects) was more popular than I thought.

We talked about how we waded in the creek behind my parents' house in Memphis. I didn't recommend this to my sons, but this was a story I shared with them. Stories like these fascinate small children. From spinning tops in a large circle drawn in the bare earth, to wearing out our blue jeans by shooting marbles on our knees, my brothers and I had fun while growing up in Memphis. These experiences were also shared with my sons. When I told them about how we thought it was good luck to catch little white butterflies, bite their heads off (another cruelty to insects incident) and run around the house three times, they screeched in disbelief. This is probably the reason they do not like bugs today. I would not recommend insect cruelty to anyone. But, I will never forget these childhood experiences. Share your adventures with your children. Smile as you watch their eyes look at you in wonderment.

I told them stories about my first real money making job of delivering newspapers when I was thirteen-years-old and living on Chicago's West Side. My brothers and I thought we were the best paperboys in the city. We had two routes in the morning and one in the afternoon. I still tell them that this was the hardest job I have ever had, but I didn't mind getting out of bed at five o'clock in the morning to deliver newspapers to my West Side neighbors.

Mama got up early to help us. My mother was usually getting ready to go to her nurse's aid job at Mount Sinai Hospital, so she could not help us with the papers. After we rolled the papers into a tight cylindrical shape, they were handed to Mama, who then put a rubber band around them. Mama would double wrap the rubber band to make sure the roll was tight. The tighter the roll the further we could throw the papers.

Some of the vestibules of the buildings where we delivered papers had such foul urine odors; we had to hold our breath. The third floor walk-ups were torturous because I could not hold my breath for the entire trip. I did not look forward to Sunday deliveries. Sunday newspapers were the largest and the heaviest. We even made the carts used to carry the newspapers during the spring, summer and fall, and the sleds used in the winter.

It is interesting how by me attempting to be the best delivery boy at a young age, my work ethic remained in the mind of someone to whom I delivered papers to fifty years ago. A high school classmate of mine visited me in Chicago in August of 2009. We reminisced about old times and Harold autographed *Friendly Enterprise*, his newly published novel about corruption in Chicago government.

Harold's family lived near my family, and I delivered newspapers to their home. Harold, who currently lives in Los Angeles, told me he informed his mother that he was going to visit me, and she immediately asked, "Wasn't he our paperboy? He was the best paperboy we ever had." The lesson in this story is, no matter what your age; attempt to be the best at whatever you are doing, whether you are a paperboy or physician. If you give it your best effort, success will eventually come. We instilled these thoughts into the brains of our sons, and they continue to study and practice to reach their number one goal of being the best musicians in the world.

During this era, along with delivering the papers, paperboys also had to collect the weekly fees from the residents. This dangerous job led to me being robbed in 1965. Roni was also robbed and cut with a short rusty knife during one of his collecting tours. I thought the six dollars I earned every week was a small fortune. Although this was a hard job, it taught me important lifelong lessons about responsibility, working, and managing money.

Demarre and Anthony laughed when I told them that I had a paper route during my sophomore year of high school. Peer pressure was rough back then, and caused me to look for another job, which I found at Allied Radio. I always had money in my pockets during my teenage years. The few dollars may not have been much, but my self-esteem was elevated as a result of the fact that I was able to earn my own money. This story was used to educate Demarre and Anthony about the importance of dedication and hard work.

Ira Carol and I always told our sons that they were winners no matter what the situation. We told them that in life, they would not always be the best in the classroom, on the basketball or tennis courts, in a Tae Kwon Do tournament, swimming class, or in a music competition, but they should always strive to be the best that they can be, no matter what the endeavor. Our goal was to teach them to always give their best effort. In our hearts, they will always be number one.

As parents, we attempted to develop strong young men, both mentally and physically. We accomplished this by being with them as often as possible without smothering them, by supporting and giving them the love and positive reinforcement that all children need.

Love is the best gift a parent can give a child. By showing them love, you give the emotional ingredient necessary for a positive and successful life. The child's life long journey starts here. The love returned by children makes life worth living. To me, it seems that these three words; love, life, and living, are indistinguishable. One cannot exist without the other. Sometimes love comes in the form of a hand written note, a long letter, a big hug, or a nice pair of expensive gym shoes.

Don't be afraid to be parents. Dr. Sharon Hicks-Bartlett, a long time friend of my family, and one who many years ago, motivated me to write this book and guided me through the process, once said: "People are afraid to be parents–they want to be their child's friend. If you raise them well, they will be your friend forever."

Parenting is serious business, and is the most important job any parent will ever have. Your child's life depends on you being the best parent–not friend–that you can be.

Demarre and Anthony were always involved in activities outside of our home. We tried to keep their minds and bodies active. Although music was just one of these activities, their music making is bringing joy to thousands of people around the world.

From Mrs. Croom's and Mrs. Ward's piano classes when they were six and seven-years-old, to music lessons in the homes of Mrs. Levitin and Mr. Green, tennis at the health club, swimming at the local YMCA and Chicago State University, to music classes at the Merit School of Music, Sherwood Conservatory of Music, DePaul University, Interlochen Center for the Arts, Curtis Institute of Music and The Juilliard School, their active schedule served four primary purposes:

Provided recreational and fun activities
Provided educational opportunities and environments
Provided physical activities which kept their bodies in shape
Kept them off the streets of Chicago's South Side

On June 10, 1998, during an interview session on CNN's *Larry King Show*, the great golfer Tiger Woods stated, "Parents should provide children with opportunities–sports, music, etc." Tiger did not have any children at the time of this quote, but he understood the importance of parents providing opportunities for their children, as his parents did for him.

Ira Carol and I provided Demarre and Anthony with many opportunities, one of which was music. With our help and guidance, great teachers, and their determination and passion, they turned this early activity into professional careers. When they were very young, we observed that they showed an uncanny aptitude for music and we searched and found the best music teachers for them. If they had not been exposed to music while they were children, our sons may have never thought about music being a possible career choice.

We believed in exposing our sons to various activities. Exposure is one of the main keys that parents should use to educate their children. Finding the best teachers for them is another important key, which must be used to educate them.

We did not plan to raise two professional musicians. This was not a goal of ours. Ira Carol and I felt that it was necessary to expose them to as many activities as possible. Because of our presence during most of these classes, we watched as their interest in music grew into a passion. I am proud to say my wife and I were there every step of the way. We picked them up and hugged them when they fell down, and when they were successful, whether the accomplishments were big or small.

When it comes to these outside activities, don't be a drop off parent. Do not drop them off at the front door of the park field house and pick them up later. You must be there with your children and use these opportunities to show that you sincerely care about their well-being and success.

Children get satisfaction out of knowing that mom, dad, or other relatives and friends are watching them perform or compete. When they are successful, they will make eye contact with you. The positive non-verbal communication that takes place during the few seconds of this eye contact is invaluable and lasts a lifetime. This visual and mental bonding is a beautiful expression of love between parent and child.

If he is not successful, your child might not make eye contact with you. After the game, recital, or school play, he may walk toward you with his head down–looking at the floor. Don't just grab his hand and walk out. Stoop down and kiss him on his forehead. Give him a big hug and some words of encouragement. This emotional bonding helps to rebuild your child's self-esteem and will cause him to lift his head. You might even see him smile again. Don't neglect to say, "I love you." Can you imagine what goes through a child's mind after hitting a game-winning three pointer during a basketball game, and mom and dad are not there. In this day and age, because of cell phone and small video cameras, parents will probably see the shot after the fact, maybe on YouTube. Mom and dad will talk about that great shot for decades to come. To experience these game-winning shots, parents, grandparents, guardians, and friends, you must be there with your sons and daughters.

Sitting down and watching that twenty or thirty-year-old digital image will be priceless. I recently spent three weeks in front of my improvised basement studio, digitizing the hundreds of old cassette and VHS tapes of our sons. Watching and listening to these treasures brought tears to my eyes and a huge smile to my face. I can appreciate these treasures because I was there with them. I was in the maternity ward when they were born. Ira Carol and I saw them take their first steps. We saw the winning shots, the first swimming strokes, the first music lessons, the first recitals, and all the award presentations. We saw Demarre's high Tae Kwon Do kick to his opponent's head to win a match. We saw Anthony hit his first shot during his school's basketball game. What if he misses the shot? Coaches and teammates may try to console him, but they may also react negatively to the miss. When he swings at a high fastball and misses to end the championship game, fathers, mothers, and friends, you need to be there. When he smacks that high fastball over the center field fence to win the game, you need to be there. When he pronounces and spells that tongue twisting, mind-boggling twelve letter word to win the citywide spelling bee, you need to be there. You also need to be there when he strikes out or misspells the word. A parent's presence during these times is crucial for the mental well-being of a child. Daddy needs to be there, mama too.

*Demarre, Anthony, their grandmother Loretta Edwards,
and Ira Carol after a music recital.*

Be there with your child during the triumphs and the let-downs. The trust that is built during these times will help the child develop a well-balanced personality, and strengthens his character. It also lets him know that he has a built in parental support system, which all young children so desperately need during the formative years of their lives.

Do not neglect to be there with and for your child. You might be tired from a long day at work, or want to use Saturday and Sunday as a time to just relax, or to watch a few ball games, but you need to force yourself to spend quality time with your child. It's a must-do situation that is vital to the positive development of all of your children.

# CHAPTER EIGHT

## NOTES THAT SAY I LOVE YOU

D on't miss the opportunity to praise your children. The words, "you performed beautifully, keep up the good work, or out-standing job," helps motivate them to work harder, and demonstrate to them that you care. A pat on the back or a hug is more than a positive physical touch, which all humans need, especially during the infant and childhood stages of their lives. It is a touch that says, "I love you."

## *SPEAK*

*Speak not to me of being a mother*
*For I am not*
*Speak not of me being a parent*
*For I will stop*
*Speak not to me of sharing*
*For I have nothing to give*
*Speak to me with Love*
*And I will be all of the above*
*Ira Carol, April 12, 1994*

Besides the hugs and kisses, it is not a bad idea to write positive reinforcing letters or notes to your children. If you provide them with paper, pencils, and crayons, they will also write you notes and draw fantastic pieces of art. Sometimes they will write these notes or drawings on the walls and doors of your home. Don't freak out and don't panic. Take a photo of the drawings and photograph your child while he is cleaning the wall or door. Use these experiences as teaching tools. I guarantee that you will laugh when you look at these old pictures twenty-five or fifty years later. You will laugh even louder and harder when you view them with your adult child later in life.

These are teachable moments when they happen and even more precious when viewed decades later. During these later viewing sessions, make sure you have some tissue or a hankie nearby for an unforced tear or two will definitely fall. Tears of joy never stop flowing and never dry up. My tears continue to flow and irrigate the huge smiles that emanate from the past and present thoughts of my sons.

Today I played with my racing car set, my brother
and I put it together. We watched cartoons too, but we
did clean up. I wore my new Coca-Cola shirt with blue

pants. We played monopoly for three hours. I watched cartoons, I drew things, and I wrote my journal. I had lots of fun playing with my racing track. We went to the movies to see The Last Emperor.
Anthony McGill, 8-years-old
Journal Entry December 26, 1987

When Demarre was eleven-years-old, he left a note on his mother's pillow. "I love you when you work out." Demarre knew that his mother had a serious workout regimen when he was younger, and when she started exercising after taking a few years off; he left this short note for her. This show of affection motivated Ira Carol to invite several friends to work out with her in the basement of our home. This was the start of a weekly exercise program.

Parents should use note cards purchased at the local store as motivational tools. Teachers use little smiley face stickers, parents should use them also. Write little love notes or other positive thoughts on pieces of driftwood or flat rocks collected during that walk along the riverbank or beach. Be creative and have fun as you teach your children.

Use whatever tools available to motivate and teach your sons and daughters. Many of the simple things around you can be used to teach lifelong lessons. Find and use them every day. You do not have to wait until your child does something great, does well in school, or wins a gymnastics or Tae Kwon Do competition before you give him a card with an, "I love you" note in it.

Fathers, don't be afraid to tell your sons and daughters, "I love you." If you truly love your children, tell them. Don't fall into the trap of believing that you are less of a man if you show affection toward your children. Don't think that you will emasculate your son by verbally expressing your affection toward him. He is your child. Let him know that you love him. My sons are strong young men and I still say to them, "I love you." Demarre and Anthony do

not hesitate to tell Ira Carol and me that they love us. We started expressing our love to our children the day they were born and will continue until we are no longer walking the earth. It makes me feel great when my sons say to me, "I love you daddy." At age sixty-three, when I hear these words of affection from my sons, I still have to reach into my back pocket for my handkerchief. I always keep some clean ones handy, just in case.

Start to use the word love around your children from the day they are born and don't stop. Explain to them what the word means. You will be pleasantly surprised when you receive those little "Love" notes from your children.

106

Ira Carol and I didn't throw any of Demarre's or Anthony's writings, drawings, or certificates away. Actually, we didn't throw away anything related to our children, although some of the treasures were lost years ago when our basement flooded. The many plastic storage cases filled with these treasures will provide us with a lifetime of joyful smiles and tears of joy.

On February 16, 2010, I found a poem Demarre wrote in 1984:

## LOVE

*Love is sharing things with each other*
*Love is caring and taking care of each other*
*Love is a strong, delicate force, which comes into you after you have met*
someone
*Love is easy to find, but hard to stay with*
*If you do find it you are blessed*
*If you don't, you have a whole lifetime left*
*The lucky ones have a chance to be a friend of love*
*The unlucky ones have the chance to be in the warmth of themselves*
*If there is no love, there is no life*
*No love means no wife*
*No love means no groom*
*Demarre Lavelle McGill*
*December 18, 1984*
*Nine-years-old*

On December 25, 2011, Ira Carol, Demarre, Anthony, and I were sitting at the dinner table in our South Side home; preparing to feast on a ten-course meal prepared by my wife and me. Demarre was asked to say a prayer of blessings on this special day. He hesitated a few seconds–surprised that his mother asked him to bless the food–then delivered a short but beautiful prayer of thanksgiving. He ended the blessing with the words, "I love you."

# A FATHER'S TRIUMPHANT STORY

Demarre smiled and stated that when he is speaking to audiences attending his *Art of Élan* concerts, he finishes his comments with the words, "I love you." "The audiences have come to expect me to say these three words," he said. Demarre learned to use these words early in his life. He was also taught their meaning and continues to use them to this day.

Place one of those smiley face stickers on her book bag before she goes to school. Place a "keep up the good work" note on her pillow before she goes to bed. For those special accomplishments, it's okay to go ahead and spend that extra money on a good pair of gym shoes. Be prepared to spend well over one hundred dollars. For those special occasions or accomplishments, it's worth the cost.

The following is a letter I wrote to Demarre and Anthony on May 1, 1996:

> To Demarre Lavelle and Anthony Barrone McGill:
> As you know, Phil Jackson is the coach of the Chicago Bulls and is considered one of the best coaching minds in the business. I personally think he is a genius.
> When I read the following, I thought about you guys, in that you dudes seem to think like Phil Jackson! The following appeared in the *Chicago Sun-Times* sports section on April 28, 1996:
> Motivation: Before game 1 Friday night, Jackson taped a Walt Whitman poem on the lockers of all the players:
> 'Henceforth we seek not good fortune. We ourselves are good fortune.'
> Jackson explained his selection and the reasoning behind the timing of the message.
> Well, it's a long week. You sit around for five or six days and you wait, he said. You talk about the laurels of

108

a 70-win season and all that. You get a lot of pats on the back and good wishes and then you have time to think about maybe, you know, maybe we're lucky and maybe it's going to be tough in the playoffs and you get anxious.

You have to realize who you are and what brought you to this point.

The message: We're not lucky, we're good.

Heat coach Pat Riley also got into the words-of-wisdom approach, telling his team before they left for Chicago:

The first step in winning is believing you can win.

*(4-28-96, Chicago Sun-Times)*

Love,

Daddy

Demarre was twenty and Anthony was sixteen-years-old when I sent them this letter. As a caring parent, never stop motivating your children, no matter what age they are.

Sometimes during the arduous task of raising children, those little notes they will leave you won't all be positive ones. Parents must realize that children are human beings and have emotions that sometimes are expressed negatively. Seize upon these emotional times to teach.

The following is a letter Demarre wrote to his mother and me in 1991:

(I left this here on purpose!)

Dear People,

You will never take my mind, my Katie, or my music away from me!

Demarre Lavelle McGill

Excerpt from <u>Me</u>

by Demarre Lavelle McGill

Ira Carol and I don't recall what motivated him to write us this short letter, but I used it as an opportunity to teach. In response to his letter, I wrote the following to Demarre on November 25, 1991. He was sixteen-years-old at the time.

> Dear People:
> No! I can't call you people because I know who you are, you're Demarre Lavelle McGill, my son!
> Dear son:
> I read your note, which you left in the van on purpose. I also left this note on purpose, for it seems that every attempt at small talk, or every attempt to carry on a normal conversation ends in some type of family feud.
> Take the time each day to thank God for what He has given you in your short life. Take the time each day to thank your parents (yes, your mother and your father) for what we have given you. You are what you are today, not just because of Demarre Lavelle McGill, but because of God's plan for your life and your parents' and friends' uncompromising support.
> As your father, I have given you (believe it or not), much more than I can ever take away. If nothing else, I along with your mother have given you love, direction, encouragement, and support in practically all of your endeavors. As your father, why would I want to take anything away from you? If you were on drugs, hanging out on the corner, unfocused, living a negative life, and at the same time living in our house, yes, I would attempt to take something away from you (change your behavior). I guess childhood rebellion is somewhat normal, but for your own sake, don't turn on your parents, for with all the talent you have, you still have a long way to go before you reach adulthood and have true independence. No

matter what you think, I am willing to continue this support if you allow me to, for you are my son and I love you.

On your note you wrote, 'Excerpt from Me by Demarre Lavelle McGill.' Is this a book you are working on? I have noticed on other occasions when I say something you don't like, you take out your paper and pencil and start writing. This is good. Is there anything positive about me in your writings? I wonder...

Again, you used the words 'Excerpt from Me by Demarre Lavelle McGill.' Don't ever forget about some other very important words in the English language... US, WE, OTHERS, GOD, and FAMILY.

Open up your mind and attempt to empathize with others. Sometimes try to understand that, 'no man is an island' *(John Donne)*, and that we are all interrelated in the sense that WE becomes more important than ME.

I would not think about attempting to take something away from you, but as your father, and as long as you live in this household, I will continue to set certain guidelines or regulations, which I think will help in your quest to be the best. You know that in 16 years, there have been very few rules or regulations placed on you. We could have been much more restrictive, but we allowed you to pursue your music with basically no strings attached, which has helped you reach the heights you have reached.

Lavelle, whatever you do, don't get so paranoid to the point that you start thinking that your family is out to get you. There are enough people in this world who will try to take your mind and everything else, and for you to waste valuable time and energy rebelling unnecessarily against your father is indeed a waste. You once told me you believe in good. You should also believe in

GOD, for the two are inseparable anyway, and you cannot have one without the other. Furthermore, believe in your mother, your father, and your brother, because as they say, 'blood is thicker than water,' and our love will always be there no matter what the situation.

In closing, please remember that the words I and ME are the smallest words in the dictionary, and WE and US, to a certain degree, are the largest.

'Together we stand, divided we fall,' and remember, nobody is perfect.

Love,

Daddy

Our little testosterone battle didn't last long. In a short time we were communicating normally, as fathers and sons should. Parents must realize that every moment and every situation is full of opportunity for teaching. If I had allowed this situation to grow by responding in a negative manner, or by not responding at all, the problem could have grown exponentially and could have changed our relationship forever.

Parents, don't allow this to happen. Take control of the situation and turn it into a positive teachable moment. Throughout the forty plus years of our relationship, Ira Carol and I also wrote letters, notes, and sent each other greeting cards to express our feelings. Most of these writings and cards were positive and were used to express congratulations for various accomplishments, or just to say, "I love you." A few of them were used to "break the ice" when we were having problems communicating with each other.

Our marriage has not been flawless. We had our disagreements and arguments along the way, but through verbal or non-verbal communication, and through letters, notes, and text messages, we overcame obstacles, which all married couples face.

Don't neglect to write positive letters and notes to your child. If he has a cell phone, send him a "keep up the good work" text message every now and then. These communication tools are important keys, which can be used in the process of raising your children, and never neglect to "show them some love."

*1972 photo of me holding my pawnshop flute,*
*a 1969 birthday gift from Ira Carol.*

# CHAPTER NINE

## E-G-B-D-F AND THE NEW F-A-C-E
## ON MY PAWN SHOP FLUTE

In 1969, Ira Carol took the train to a downtown pawnshop and bought me a metal flute for my 19th birthday. I called this instrument a "real flute," compared to the wooden ones my brothers and I played during the late 1960s and 70s. The only thing I didn't like about this instrument was its pink and beige synthetic leather case.

The Martin Busine Corporation manufactured this flute. I remember asking Ira Carol, "How much did you pay for it?" After hesitating a few seconds, she finally said, *"Ninety dollars."* This was big money back then, and I thought my slightly tarnished flute to be the greatest gift I had ever received. I was able to force a sound out of it immediately and the following week, I rushed downtown and bought two paperback training manuals relative to playing the flute. My goal was to teach myself how to play it. I still have the one entitled, *Flute and Piccolo Method, Book 1,* by Donald J. Pease, published by Pro Art Publications, Inc. This book is now over forty years old. Although I enjoyed improvising on my new flute, it ended up collecting dust on a closet shelf until Demarre found the instrument and started playing with it.

In an October 6, 2011 article in the *Seattle Times,* Michael Upchurch writes about Demarre McGill:

> McGill began playing the flute in Chicago when he was seven-years-old; starting with a used silver flute his mother gave his father before Demarre was born. 'I loved it immediately,' he says of the flute. 'My father just said, blow across it like you blow across a coke bottle.' And that was my first lesson, I guess. For seven years after that... I would have these moments of passion. I couldn't stop practicing, and then I would just plateau. Then I would have another moment of musical ecstasy...

Demarre seemed excited about finding my old flute, and it didn't take long for him to produce sounds from it. I don't know if they could be called beautiful, but these initial experimental sounds from my "real flute" were music to my ears. None of us knew that this instrument would influence the direction of his life forever.

We didn't know until October of 2010 that Demarre and I had similar thoughts about the pink case. "I wanted to use black spray paint on it," he said. It is amazing that my improvisations on a wooden flute as a teenager would ultimately play a role in my sons

*My brother-in-law Sheldon, Roni, a friend, and me playing around
in our South Side basement. About 1977. McGill family photo.*

becoming professional musicians, and members of major symphony orchestras and chamber ensembles.

I knew that this instrument now belonged to my son and it was
time to find him a teacher. Mr. Robert Green, who was Demarre's
first private flute teacher, lives on the street south of our home.
He is a classically trained flute player who teaches and performs in
the Chicago area. Mr. Green was founder and General Manager
of the Chatham Village Symphony Orchestra and the Masterworks
Woodwind Quintet.

I still remember the first assignment Mr. Green gave Demarre.
He had to learn the notes representing the lines and spaces on the
musical staff, E-G-B-D-F (Every Good Boy Does Fine) representing the lines, and F-A-C-E representing the spaces. I accompanied
Demarre to most of these early lessons and attempted to learn
music theory along with him. I quickly lost interest and decided

*Anthony, Demarre, Ira Carol, and Mr. Barry Elmore.*
*Courtesy of Delores Kohl Foundation.*

that I would leave the music making to my son and Mr. Green. The act of teaching myself how to play the flute did not last long. I soon stored the books on my bedroom closet shelf and continued to improvise on my wooden ones.

Demarre was a good student and quickly learned the musical concepts taught by Mr. Green. At this young age, he was very serious about practicing and studying at home. He worked with Mr. Green from 1983 through 1986. Knowing the importance of supporting our children, my wife or I was always there with him.

One day after a lesson, Mr. Green said to me, "Demarre has progressed to the point where I think you need to find another teacher for him." The strong musical foundation established in Mr. Green's South Side home was as solid as the concrete walls of his basement, and was a major factor in helping Demarre become the musician he is today. Ira Carol and I always attempted to find the best teachers and schools for our sons. Although we had no idea that they would someday become professional musicians, the positive educational environments and great teachers helped them reach many of their short and long-range goals.

After Mr. Green, Demarre studied at the Merit Music Program with Ms. Cindy Gdalman; Mrs. Carol Morgan at the American Conservatory of Music; and with Mrs. Susan Levitin, who taught flute in her home and at the Sherwood Conservatory of Music. Mrs. Levitin had perhaps the greatest influence on Demarre's early musical life. He studied with her from 1987 until 1992, when he moved to Philadelphia, Pennsylvania to study with Julius Baker and Jeffrey Khaner at the world-renowned Curtis Institute of Music.

> Today my brother had to go to flute practice at All City Band, it's a long practice. I brought a book to keep me busy. After, I went to my cousin's house. We played with the toys. We had a lot of fun.
> Anthony Barrone McGill, 8-years-old

During an interview with *The Chamber Music Society of Lincoln Center*, Demarre said:

> My teachers have had an enormous influence on my music. When I was growing up in Chicago, I was very fortunate to have teachers who knew when to 'give me to someone else.' The teacher I studied with the longest in Chicago, Susan Levitin, was an unbelievable motivator. She encouraged me to work extremely hard, but always seemed to allow me to be a kid. My two teachers at Curtis, Julius Baker and Jeffrey Khaner were both amazing. Mr. Khaner made me realize that 'talent' could be dangerous. Consistency, discipline, and hard work became more important the more talent you have. Mr. Baker is definitely my favorite flutist. Just being around him was a learning experience for me. Every time I walked out of a lesson, I

had a very clear picture of just how much work I needed to do to be 2% as great as he is. *(Chamber Music Society Website)*

Demarre's first flute solo performance was at Blackwell African Methodist Episcopal Zion Church located at 39th and Langley Avenue on the South Side of Chicago. This big grey stone church was two city blocks from the public housing high-rise building my father lived in when he first moved to Chicago from Memphis, Tennessee.

My mother and father were divorced, but my brothers and sisters visited daddy periodically. Because the elevators in this building seemed to always be broken, we had to walk up to my father's small two-bedroom apartment where he lived with his other family. Walking those five flights was chilling. The boys who hung out near the elevators did not smile at strangers. We were infringing on their territory and they did not like this. Their deep-seated stares were as penetrating as the sharp needles nurses used to vaccinate us when we lived in Memphis. We didn't have any physical problems navigating those stairs, but the thoughts of us getting beaten up by the neighborhood boys were scary. My brothers and sisters survived the visits to my father's apartment. A few years ago, those high-rise projects were torn down and replaced by expensive brick two-story duplexes and single-family homes.

Reverend Riddick was the pastor of Blackwell Church, and in 1983, he and other members organized an Easter Sunday program. Members of the Sunday school class knew that Demarre was taking flute lessons and asked him to perform during the program.

Demarre taught himself the Sarah Flower Adams hymn, *Nearer My God to Thee,* and the great Negro National Anthem, *Lift Every Voice and Sing,* written by James Weldon Johnson. I remember listening to him while he was practicing these pieces. "Very good. You hit one bad note in there," I explained. Demarre responded: "Uh, uh, that was the same note except it was low. The audience won't notice that though. That was just a low note." Sometimes he got angry with me when I made suggestions on how he could improve his playing. Demarre knew that I could not read music and had no formal training on how to play an instrument. To me he was saying, "I got this daddy. I'm the only musician in this family." I backed away from Demarre and allowed him to learn the pieces on his own terms.

We recorded several of Demarre's practice sessions and still have one of the tapes. We listen to it periodically whenever we want to reminisce and have a couple of good laughs. The text from the above training session came from one of these cassette tape recordings. The live performance at the church was beautiful and Demarre received a standing ovation. After the performance, we could see the joy on Demarre's face. Experiences like this help to build self-esteem in children and remind me of my childhood when my brothers and sisters recited poems during various church programs. This performance motivated Demarre to practice more and helped him realize that he could influence people through his music making. I'm sure the five-dollar bill Reverend Riddick gave him after the performance also motivated him. The five-dollar donations soon turned to ten. He liked this.

> Today we went to church. At church we had a Christmas program. The program was a good one. We each said something about Christmas. After the program a person from the church fixed us pizza.
> Anthony Barrone McGill, 8-years-old
> Journal Entry, 12-20-87

One of the most important things a parent can do for their child is to find the best teachers possible. Parents must also recognize when it is time to find another school or teacher for the student because he has learned all he can from a particular teacher.

Ira Carol and I were fortunate to have had good babysitters for our sons. In most cases they were family members; Ira Carol's mother and grandmother, my sister's mother-in-law Mrs. Woodson,

Mrs. Jones, and Mama Norris. The care these beautiful women gave, allowed us to go to work every day so we could provide for our children and ourselves. We tried a couple of commercial day care centers, but after Demarre came home with skin and scalp infections, we went back to family care.

Starting in the second grade, Demarre attended Edgar Allan Poe Classical School in Chicago. Poe Classical is a local Magnet school where students are tested before being admitted. Poe is located on the far South Side of Chicago. This majestic looking building always resembled a fort to me, but was considered one of the best elementary schools in the city. The school educated some of the top students in Chicago, including Tempest Bledsoe, a member of the *Cosby Show* cast for many years.

Ira Carol and I were always concerned about the quality of education being offered in the public schools of Chicago. Because of the high standardized test scores of students at Poe Classical, she completed an application in her attempt to get Demarre into this school. She started this process late during the summer.

At the beginning of the school year, we enrolled Demarre in another elementary school near our home while we waited for the Poe results. This school was closer to our home than Poe Classical, but standardized test scores were much lower than the scores of Poe students.

Two weeks after enrolling him in the local school, we were informed that based upon his test scores and the fact that there was an opening; Demarre was accepted into Poe Classical. We were overjoyed because of the large number of students who were attempting to fill the limited number of vacancies at the school, and the fact that students were picked up from their homes and bussed to and from school every day, at no cost to the parents.

Poe Classical had good academic programs and teachers, and a band and choir program run by Mr. Barry Elmore. He taught basic music fundamentals to beginning music students and conducted the band, which consisted of more advanced instrumentalist. Mr. Elmore positively influenced thousands of students during his teaching career.

# DEMARRE MCGILL

*Original members of the Chicago Teen Ensemble.*

To become a member of the band at Poe, students were required to be in the fourth grade or higher, have basic knowledge of music theory, and the ability to play a musical instrument. During the second and third grades, Demarre studied theory, was a member of the school choir, and later joined the All-City Elementary School Chorus. Initially, he did not like singing, but eventually came to enjoy this activity. Each week, Demarre seemed to have fun during the rehearsals and performances.

Demarre's first instrument at this school was a recorder, which was similar to the wooden wind instruments my brothers and I played when we were teenagers. The recorder is a plastic instrument used by music teachers to teach beginning music students.

While a student at Poe Classical, Demarre was introduced to another important person who influenced his life. Vanessa Hill was a second grader at Poe and was a very talented violin player. We met Vanessa after her solo performance during the school's yearly music concert. Vanessa played a classical piece for solo violin. She looked like a little angel standing on stage in her floor length white dress. Her performance was outstanding. After meeting Vanessa and her mother, Mrs. Nancy Hill, Ira Carol and I knew that we wanted our son to someday perform on stage in front of an audience, although we had no aspirations of Demarre becoming a professional musician. Several years later, while in their teens, Demarre and Vanessa became charter members of a group called the Chicago Teen Ensemble, which included Andrea Hargrave, Lenae Harris, Kelli and Traci English, Anaya McMurray, and other Poe Classical student musicians. Later, Anthony became the youngest member of the Teen Ensemble. This group of young African American classical musicians was the brainchild of Mr. Barry Elmore, Mrs. Nancy Hill, and the late Mrs. Farrow Hargrave, and continued to perform classical music in the Chicago area for many years after Demarre graduated from Poe. All of the original members of the group are now adults. Several are married, raising their own families, and pursuing various professional careers. This exemplifies the importance of exposing children to other children who have strong, loving family environments, and are involved in positive activities within and outside of their homes and schools.

Demarre was eleven-years-old when he wrote his first musical composition while we were members of Blackwell Church. This was a short piece called *Magic*. As a means of teaching Demarre and Anthony about the copyright process, Ira Carol and I secured a government copyright on *Magic*. We explained to them what a copyright was and the importance of protecting the piece from unauthorized use by others. We liked the piece and wanted to protect it, but we also used this process as a teaching tool for our sons. During our child-raising years, Ira Carol and I attempted to find every opportunity possible to teach our sons.

*Copy of Demarre's original Magic composition.*

Demarre performed *Magic* on a piano during another Sunday school program at Blackwell Church. I am not sure if Reverend Riddick gave him another five or ten dollars, but all the people in the church sanctuary stood up and loudly expressed their joy after hearing his playing. After the performance, Demarre smiled as he shyly returned to his seat next to his mother and brother. All of us were proud of Demarre. Anthony seemed to be more excited than any of the people in the audience. Just like me and his mother, he was proud of his big brother.

While at home during the 2001 Thanksgiving holiday, Demarre was searching through a storage box containing some of his old music papers and found the original copy of *Magic*. Demarre and Anthony both came home during the 2009 Christmas holiday. One of my sons found a cassette tape of Demarre playing *Magic* on his electric keyboard.

We were all impressed at the quality of the sound from the old tape and the artistry of the piece. We listened to *Magic* many times before Demarre and Anthony returned to their homes in San Diego and New York City respectively.

Although parents need to seek out and provide the best teachers for their children, they must remember above all, they are their children's first teachers and should be the best teachers. Use every opportunity to teach them. The child's entire being will act like a natural sponge which soaks up all the positive stuff dished out by parents, teachers and others. Be aware that they also soak up all of the negatives they are exposed to.

A natural sponge is very porous marine animal, and seems to be more permeable and durable than synthetic ones. Sponges of all types, when placed in or on liquids, will soak up the liquid to a point where they become supersaturated. Children are like these sponges. They soak up all things around them. They absorb all the positive or negative images or stimuli they come into contact with. In loving home environments, children become saturated with beneficial things, which in turn helps them develop into positive and successful young adults.

As a parent, be aware that whatever your child is exposed to plays a role in his overall growth and development. Don't allow your child's young age to cloud the fact that his mind works like a sponge. If a child is removed from the watery environment of his mother's womb (birth), he will absorb all positive or negative, verbal, non-verbal, visual, or physical stimuli around.

Children absorb negatives or positives before they are born until the day they die. Parents, understand this, and take the necessary steps to expose your children to positive environments and make a 100% effort to keep all negatives out of their lives.

Ira Carol and I never liked spanking our sons. We recently discussed this subject and it was difficult remembering the times that we actually spanked them. We remembered one incident when Demarre was in fourth grade. He was not honest with us about his progress in one of his classes. Demarre told us that he wasn't having any problems in this class, and that all assignments had been turned in. After a conference with his teacher, we learned that missing assignments caused Demarre's low grade. We were extremely upset with him and conferred with Mr. Elmore, who advised us to not punish him by taking away any music-related activities.

Mr. Elmore saw the anger on our faces and stated, "That is not a good form of punishment." We took his advice, but we did spank him. We could not remember any times when we spanked Anthony. I am sure that we occasionally whacked them on their butts with our hands, which didn't hurt them at all physically, but embarrassed them when we were in public.

We attempted to find creative methods of disciplining our sons, such as, no dessert after a meal, no movies, and no video games or toys. Not allowing them to come out of their bedrooms unless they were going to the bathroom was another tool we used. We didn't allow them to talk on the telephone. The basketball hoop and geodesic dome in the backyard were off limits. The restrictions we placed on these backyard activities probably hurt them the most.

Violence never dominated our household. We attempted to raise our children in a non-violent environment. Even when Ira Carol and I argued, we concealed this from them and we never had physical fights. We constantly told our sons, "Positive Thinking Creates a Strong Mind, Body and Soul." Ira Carol and I tried to portray these positive thoughts and actions around our sons.

As an art teacher in the Chicago Public School system, and an active oil painter during this time, many of my artworks included the words positive thinking or think positively. Some of these paintings were sold to relatives and friends, or hung in locations throughout our home. Our sons saw these paintings every day. Our home environment was enriched by these positive images, and our constant verbalizing the importance of thinking this way, had a profound and constructive effect on our sons.

MuDear played a major role in Demarre's early life as a musician. In 1985, the Poe Classical School band was invited to perform during a *Picasso Music Program* recital at the Richard J. Daley Civic Center in downtown Chicago. MuDear and I drove Demarre downtown, and attended this performance. During a featured solo by Demarre, his old Martin Busine flute could not produce a certain musical note. He tried several times, but his flute would not make the sound he wanted. My mother hit me in the side with her elbow and whispered in my ear, "Buy that boy a flute."

Subsequently, on January 2, 1986, Demarre, Ira Carol and I visited Quinlan & Fabish, a local music instrument store located on 79th Street. We examined several of their flutes, and thought the prices were ridiculously high. The most reasonably priced one cost three hundred and thirty-six dollars. I felt that this was too much money to pay for an instrument for someone as young as Demarre. He was ten-years-old at the time.

Reluctantly, we purchased this Gemeinhardt flute for him. The smile on Demarre's face showed how excited he was about getting a brand new flute. My mother, who is no longer with us physically, was proud as any grandmother could be after we told her that Demarre had a new flute. "I can't wait to hear him play," she said.

MuDear only got a chance to hear Demarre a couple of times before her death in 1988. I am sure she heard him perform beautifully at her funeral, for she passed away only two weeks after being diagnosed with brain cancer. The Glioblastoma Multiform tumor took my mother's life so quickly it was difficult for my family to understand. She was only sixty-three-years-old. My mother's sudden death shocked everyone who knew her.

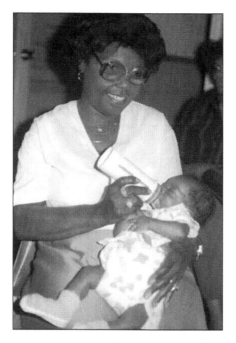

*MuDear feeding Anthony in 1979.*

Demarre's playing of the popular song *Memories* at her funeral brought tears to the eyes of everyone in the packed church in Memphis, Tennessee, and two days later at another memorial service at Taylor Funeral Home in Chicago. My mother did not get a chance to witness the impact she had on her grandson's career, but her elbow punch to the right side of my rib cage changed his life forever. This brand new flute was one of the best monetary investments we had ever made in our son. Not only did his music related study habits take on a more serious tone, there was a tremendous improvement in the quality of his sound. This new instrument caused Demarre's confidence level to soar.

The second flute we bought Demarre was purchased from Eugene S. Gordon Woodwinds on May 1, 1990. This Armstrong flute cost seven hundred ninety-seven dollars. Again, Ira Carol and

I thought this was a huge price to pay for a fourteen-year-old. The cost of the first three flutes was minuscule compared to the price of Demarre's fourth instrument.

In 1992, after packing our bags and loading our car, we began our one thousand mile journey to Massachusetts, in search of that *magic flute*. This state is the home of Brannen Brothers Flutes and Verne Powell Flutes. These companies were considered to be two of the top flute makers in America. After a long tiresome drive through Indiana, Ohio, Pennsylvania, and New York, we finally arrived at the Brannen Brothers factory. Mr. Brannen met us as we walked into the front section of his shop. After introductions, Mr. Brannen said, "Why don't you play something for me?" Demarre said, "Okay," and carefully assembled his flute, as if he was preparing for a big concert. He played a short piece for us. Mr. Brannen was surprised and excited after hearing such quality playing from someone as young as Demarre. He said, "That was great, would you like to take a tour of the factory to see how we make our instruments?"

The guided tour was fascinating. To see how these beautiful instruments are made was an awesome learning experience for my family. After leaving Brannen Brothers, we visited Powell Flutes so Demarre could try some of their popular instruments. After much debate, on May 29, 1992, we ended up buying Powell Flute body #8454. The body of the instrument cost six thousand two hundred and thirty dollars. We had already purchased the head joint from Powell for $1320.00 on July 5, 1991. Before Demarre reached the age of seventeen, Ira Carol and I had spent $8,679.00 on three flutes.

Three weeks before we purchased Demarre's flute body from Powell, we bought a Leblanc Concerto Model clarinet for Anthony. This clarinet was purchased from International Musical Suppliers for $1,900. Anthony was twelve-years-old at the time. We eventually realized that the investment we made in our sons' futures was money well spent.

Demarre helped to pay for this instrument with the $1930 in prize money he received as a result of winning the Illinois Young Performance Competition.

The following is a letter I wrote to Mr. Houston at Powell Flutes:

> Mr. Houston,
> Enclosed is a check for $1000.00 and a copy of a letter, which was sent to WTTW in Chicago. WTTW will be sending Powell Flutes a check in the amount of $1930.00 (arrangements made earlier).
> Earlier this year (before we purchased the Aurumite head-joint) I sent a check for $100.00 so Demarre could try several head joints. Please apply this $100.00 to the $1000.00 check enclosed and the check, which you will receive from WTTW–TV.
> We would like to apply the $3030.00, which you will receive ($1000 enclosed, $1930 from WTTW and $100 previous deposit) to the purchase of an Aurumite I Flute body.
> We hope this is sufficient to get Demarre Lavelle's name on your waiting list. We hope to have the body paid in full by the end of 1991.
> Demarre McGill

My wife and I never allowed money or lack of money to be an obstacle to our children's pursuit to be the best musicians that they could be. Raising children is expensive. The time and money spent in this endeavor will ultimately bring you and your children much success and joy later in life.

Parents, don't allow money to be an obstacle. Do whatever it takes to provide all the tools necessary to raise your children, no matter what the cost. You might have to work a part time job, or if possible, take out a second mortgage. If you have special knowledge or skills, barter your service to pay for your child's lessons, instruments, computers, or books.

To ensure that there was money available when they needed it, and to support our sons' musical endeavors, Ira Carol and I refinanced our home several times throughout the years. We purchased our Chicago home before Anthony was born, and in 2013 we are still making monthly mortgage payments on this same house.

Our child-raising techniques worked. Demarre and Anthony turned out to be two successful young men who are intelligent, well grounded, have positive mental attitudes, and are making people across the world happy through their music making.

## *MUSIC, MUSIC, MUSIC*

*As waves of sound*
*Creating tides abound*
*Splashing against your mind*
*Memories of time*
*Vibrations unfold*
*Of stories untold*
*Imagination radiating*
*Sense of experience accelerating*
*There is a constant throb of music*
*Where a message can be found*
*Listen closely and you may hear*
*All dimensions of your life*
*Very clear*

*James McGill, July 24, 1993*

*Anthony and Demarre at Interlochen Arts Camp.*

# CHAPTER TEN

## SUMMER MUSIC CAMP AND OTHER SCHOOLS

When Anthony was four-years-old he imitated his mother by dancing, no matter where he was. As he grew older he became a very good athlete, especially running track, swimming, and basketball. While on the track team, Anthony won many medals and trophies, which he proudly displayed in his bedroom.

His first basketball program was called *Itsy Bitsy Basketball*. It was fun watching the little boys handle a basketball and run up

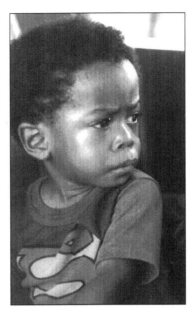

*Anthony*

and down the court, double and triple dribbling all the way. Most of the children had great fun in this program.

As with all the activities our sons participated in, either Ira Carol or I, or both of us, were there to support and encourage them. What I remember most about the various activities was the absence of fathers or adult males. In most instances, it was obvious that mothers considerably outnumbered fathers. On many occasions I was the only adult male in attendance.

Some say that the absence of supportive fathers in the African American community is a major problem, which causes many children to grow up without the support, leadership, and guidance a good father figure can provide. Based on what I have seen, I agree with this one hundred percent. Fathers must play an active role in raising their sons and daughters. I am not saying single mothers are not capable of raising successful children, for many have raised successful young males and females. I tend to think that children, who are raised in the same household by a caring father and mother, have a greater chance of growing into an emotionally and socially well-balanced and successful person. Fathers, where are you? Support your children. Give them the love, affection, and support they so desperately need.

Anthony, like his brother, attended Edgar Allan Poe Classical School. Anthony started 1st grade in September of 1985 and remained at Poe until 1987, when a strike by the Chicago public school teachers shut down the system for several weeks. During the strike, Ira Carol and I decided to transfer him to St. Thomas the Apostle, a local Catholic School that was recommended by a family friend. Our family is not Catholic. The decision to enroll Anthony in this school was based on our desire to see him in a school-learning environment and not at home. Ira Carol's thoughts and actions about transferring him to St. Thomas are as follows:

*During the third week of the strike, I talked to Anthony and tried to explain to him why we needed to find him another school. I remember he was sad that he had to leave his school and his friends. Sometime during the process of determining whether to keep Anthony at Poe, he read an article about being a protégé in a parenting magazine I had in the house.*

*While we were in my car, he told me about what he had read and said that he was a protégé. Anthony was eight-years-old at the time. His statement surprised me, although I knew he was an exceptionally smart child. The ironic thing about this conversation was the fact that I had not read the article. Later that day, I read it and told Anthony that I agreed with him.*

*I went in to speak with the Principal of St. Thomas the Apostle and was told that there were no more vacancies at her school, but she would give me an application just in case a seat became available. I completed the application while still in her office. I casually mentioned the protégé article and what Anthony had told me. I left the application on the principal's desk and left.*

*A few days later, I received a call from the school. The clerk informed me that Anthony was accepted. My husband and I were very happy about this, but neither we, nor Anthony, realized that his being accepted into St. Thomas would change his life forever!*

*Anthony playing with his toy saxophone. His cousin Marcus*
*is on the left, and cousin Eric is holding his guitar.*

In 1988 while Anthony was in 4<sup>th</sup> grade at St. Thomas the Apostle, the administrators decided to start a school band program. The school invited Quinlan and Fabish to bring in band instruments so that parents and students could view and handle them.

I took Anthony to the school that evening. He seemed to be holding back his emotions as we walked into a small, dimly lit conference room on the first floor, down the hall from the Principal's office. After advancing a few feet into the room, we paused and glanced at the instruments. Anthony originally talked to us about playing a saxophone, and that is the instrument I expected him to end up playing. I remember Anthony slowly approaching a long table draped in an off-white tablecloth. The instruments were neatly arranged on several of these tables. Other children and their parents were carefully inspecting the musical instruments and seemed to be excited about choosing one of them.

Anthony went directly to the shiny gold saxophone, placed his hands on it, and struggled to pick it up. He finally embraced the large instrument with his arms and held it close to his chest. He looked at me and said, "It's too big." Anthony seemed saddened by this revelation. I could see it in his eyes and heard it in the tone of his voice. I shook my head in agreement, took the saxophone from Anthony, and placed it gently back on the table. I tried my best not to leave any fingerprints on this beautiful new saxophone.

"Do you see any other instrument you want to play," I asked Anthony. After a couple of remorseful minutes, he approached the section of a table and picked up a long slender black and silver clarinet. He placed this instrument in his hands, looked at me, and said, "This one." His face lit up like he had found the perfect toy. "I'll try this one," he said. I again shook my head in agreement and smiled as I approached him. The smile on Anthony's face told me that this was the instrument for him. I remember this night like it was yesterday.

Sometimes in a child's early life–if given the opportunity–he will make decisions that neither he nor his parents know, will set the course for the rest of his life.

The following week, Ira Carol, Anthony, and I went to the Quinlin and Fabish store and rented a clarinet for Anthony. We didn't want to purchase the instrument for fear that he might become bored with music and quit playing.

After we returned home with the clarinet, Anthony could not put it down. He was forever hooked. He has been playing the clarinet for over two decades now, and will no doubt continue to make beautiful music with his clarinet for the rest of his life.

It is amazing to think that certain small things parents do with their child while he is young, can be long-lasting and life-changing events. Sometimes one of these early activities ends up being the child's profession. This happened to both my sons.

Anthony talked about his career and his musical abilities in an article, which appeared in *The Cincinnati Enquirer* on June 21, 2001:

> It was a gradual process. I didn't wake up one day and go Eureka! I've got it. But from the start, I felt like I really liked it. But a career? That came quite a bit later. I knew that I loved it, but for a long time, I wanted to be a lawyer.

In an October 3, 2009 article written by Richard Scheinin for *Mercury News*, Anthony stated the following:

> My parents–they're just the best, he says. They've always been super-supportive. They've always liked how I play–they weren't lying, but even as a kid they would always compliment me on how expressive I was. They're artists, and they relate to music in a very feel sort of way.

In the same article, Anthony commented about my study habits when I was a student at the Illinois Institute of Technology, and during the time I was taking exams and being promoted to various ranks within the Chicago Fire Department. In 1984, I graduated from IIT with a Masters Degree in Public Administration. During my twenty-seven year career as a member of the Chicago Fire Department, I held the following positions: firefighter, engineer, lieutenant, captain, battalion chief, deputy district chief, district chief and deputy fire commissioner. The following are Anthony's thoughts about my work ethic:

> He was always taking tests, and working really hard. I remember him days on end, just studying...

constantly. This is something that I think we saw constantly growing up. And my brother became really passionate about the flute, practicing obsessively. By the time I came along everyone was involved with something constantly. There was a lot of possibility in our house: The sky's the limit.

The *Mercury News* article ended with Anthony talking about my reaction to listening to the first draft of his inaugural CD that was released in September of 2010:

> My dad said, 'This is great. The only problem is, now we're going to be up all night listening.' Anthony continued to say: I don't even know if they realize how, to this day, it still means so much to me that they like what I'm doing. And they tell me all the time.

Anthony's main role model was his older brother. He watched Demarre practice four or five hours every day before he went to school and after he returned home. "How did it work that you became a flutist and your brother a clarinetist?" asked Jonathan Dean, a blogger with the Seattle Opera Blog. *(Meet Our Instrumentalist, March 7, 2012)* Demarre responded:

> I'm four years older, and by the time he started playing I had already been playing for six years. At that point, I was in it, I was practicing all the time and I loved it, so it kind of made sense that he would do something. And he's great; he's had great success.

Demarre and Anthony played together all the time and had few fights that I can remember. The geodesic dome and the basketball hoop in our small backyard was always the central outdoor meeting place. We spent many days picnicking on the lakefront, visiting museums, libraries or bookstores, driving them to music lessons, or driving to Woodhaven Lakes Camping Resort. The basketball hoop is probably why both of my sons still love to play basketball.

In addition to their musical studies, their outside activities and the home play time, we gave them chores to do as well. Taking out the garbage, sweeping the floors, and folding clothes were just a few of their home duties.

> Today I had to fold clothes and put them away. I was tired that day so after I finished I took a nap. I kept asking my mother if I could go over to my cousin's house, but my cousin was calling on the phone.
> Anthony Barrone McGill, 8-years-old
> Journal Entry 12-28-87

The following is a recent statement made by Anthony:

> Well, my brother, he was so—and is so—amazing, he says. He was like a rock star in Chicago when I was growing up. He has always been a teacher of mine and a supporter of mine. He was always, like, telling people, Wait till you hear my brother. He's ridiculously awesome. He'd push me up and pull me up. *(Steve Penhollow, The Journal Gazette, January 15, 2010)*

One of Anthony's first private teachers was a local jazz musician named Ronald Jackson. He was a good teacher and an active jazz musician who came to our home to teach Anthony basic music concepts. After he fell asleep during one of Anthony's lessons, Ira Carol and I decided to find a more formal music program for him. I walked into our living room where the lesson was being held and noticed that Mr. Jackson was nodding off. I called Ira Carol and said, "Check this out, Mr. Jackson is sleep." She was as shocked as I was. While we were standing there, he opened his eyes and tried to finish the lesson. This incident made us realize it was time to find Anthony another teacher.

Ira Carol visited The Sherwood Conservatory of Music where she met a clarinet teacher named Mr. Stanley Davis. Mr. Davis told her that he didn't take students as young as Anthony, who was ten-years-old at the time. My wife immediately said, *"Just listen to his playing for a few minutes."* Her strategy worked again. After hearing Anthony play, Mr. Davis accepted him as a student. Anthony studied with him for about one year. His playing and understanding of music theory improved considerably during this time.

After taking clarinet lessons for about two years, Anthony asked his mother, "Can I switch to the flute?" Ira Carol immediately asked, *"Why do you want to switch?"* Anthony responded, "I just want to play the flute like Lavelle (Demarre)." Ira Carol knew that the flute was not one of his early choices and told Anthony,*"No you can't switch."* She explained to him that he had not given her a valid reason for changing instruments. She said, *"The clarinet was your choice and you should stick with it."* Anthony went on to say that he did not think the clarinet had many solo parts written for it. Later on he found out this was untrue. He had not been playing long enough to understand there were many solo opportunities for a clarinetist. Today, I am sure Anthony appreciates the fact that his mother did not allow him to switch instruments.

As Demarre and Anthony started to gain more music related notoriety in the Chicago area, Ira Carol and I attempted to attend every recital together. I started to experience chest pains during their recitals. Visions of me having a heart attack during one of their performances sometimes rolled through my mind. After going through extensive examinations at a local hospital, my doctor informed me that he did not find any problems with my heart. He said, "You need to relax your chest muscles and don't forget to breathe when you're watching your sons perform." His advice helped. After many years of experiencing simultaneous joy and pain in the concert hall, I learned to relax, breathe, and enjoy the music. My heart still beats faster than normal when I hear them play, and so far, paramedics haven't had to carry me out of any concert halls on a stretcher.

Before studying at the Interlochen Arts Camp and Marlboro Music, Demarre and Anthony studied at The Merit Music Program, now known as Merit School of Music. Mrs. Alice S. Pfaelzer and Mrs. Emma Endres-Kountz founded this community music school in 1979.

After the Chicago Public School system dropped music from its curriculum because of financial difficulties, these two women took it upon themselves to provide music training to children. The early classes were held in donated space at Roosevelt University. As Merit started to gain support from the community and because of the ever-increasing size of the student body, the school moved to a remodeled area in the lower level of the old Dearborn Train Station at Dearborn and Polk Streets in Chicago. Today, the school is housed in a multimillion-dollar facility in Chicago's newly redeveloped west loop area.

"Merit School of Music provides high-quality music education to students in metropolitan Chicago. Its primary goals are to help young people achieve their full musical potential, to remove economic barriers to participation, and to stimulate personal and educational growth through music." *(Merit School of Music Website)*

Ira Carol and I drove Demarre and Anthony to Merit. Visiting on Saturdays was always the most exciting. It was fascinating to watch the hundreds of children moving through the corridors holding small violins, trumpets, flutes, clarinets, and other instruments. All of the children seemed to have smiles on their faces. The sounds emanating from the practice rooms coupled with the sounds and sights of the children in motion reminded me of a

*Anthony, Ira Carol, Demarre, and Duffie Adelson, President of Merit School of Music. Photo courtesy of Dr. Sharon Hicks-Bartlett.*

busy Chicago freeway. The once a year *Performathon* began in 1983. This all day recital program provided opportunities for students to perform on stage in front of an audience of over three hundred people.

Many proud parents attended *Performathon* and cheered their children after watching them perform short musical selections.

Ira Carol and I never missed our sons' performances and often attended long after they had left Merit. In 2011, Merit reached "nearly 6,000 young people" in the Chicago area–all because of the vision and efforts of two women who cared, Mrs. Alice S. Pfaelzer and Mrs. Emma Endres-Kountz.

Demarre attended Merit during the 1985-1986 season. This school had great teachers and programs for the children. Ira Carol and I wanted Demarre to continue studying flute with Mrs. Gdalman

Anthony performing at Merit. Courtesy of Merit
School of Music, Chicago, Illinois.

and attempted to register him one week after the registration period
ended. But due to the overwhelming popularity of the programs
at Merit, and the large number of students who registered before
Demarre's attempt, he was not allowed to attend. We were extremely
disappointed. After pleading with the administration, we finally realized that Demarre would not be allowed to study at the Merit Music
Program this year. This was a good learning experience for us, and
was the last time our sons missed a registration deadline.

For several years, Anthony's primary teacher at Merit was Mr. David
Tuttle. With the help of Mr. Tuttle and his other teachers, Anthony's
understanding of theory and musical concepts reached a high level.

He showed tremendous progress during the time he studied
at Merit. Because he learned so rapidly, Mrs. Pfealzer decided

*In January of 2012, Clarinetist Larry Combs visited Anthony backstage after Anthony soloed with the Metropolitan Opera Orchestra. Photo by D. McGill.*

to introduce him to Mr. Larry Combs, Principal Clarinetist with the Chicago Symphony Orchestra. Mrs. Pfealzer said to my wife, "Why don't we let Larry Combs hear him." Mrs. Pfealzer called Mr. Combs and asked if he would listen to Anthony's playing as a means of possibly taking him on as a student. Mr. Combs, who was on the faculty of DePaul University, responded, "I don't teach elementary school children." Mrs. Pfealzer responded, "I just want you to hear him." Mr. Combs did not make any promises to her, but agreed to hear Anthony play. This is another example of where persistence paid off. About a week later, Mrs. Pfealzer, Ira Carol, and Anthony drove up to DePaul University to meet with Mr. Combs. He worked with Anthony for about half an hour while Mrs. Pfealzer and my wife waited nervously in a reception area near the classroom. Later, Mr.

Combs came out of the room and stated, "I can work with Anthony." He was highly impressed by his playing. Mr. Combs also said, "When I am not available, Mrs. Julie DeRoche will be his teacher." Mrs. DeRoche was also a member of the clarinet faculty at DePaul.

Anthony studied with Mr. Combs and Mrs. DeRoche for a year and a half. During his time at DePaul, Anthony continued to take classes at the Merit Music Program. The one-on-one training he received at Merit and DePaul helped shape his musical future. His music making continued to improve, and made everyone who heard him play, marvel at his beautiful tone and phrasing. People would always rave about his young age and how great a musician he was.

In 2009, Ira Carol and I visited Anthony in New York and attended a Metropolitan Opera performance of Giuseppe Verdi's *Aida*. This production was beautiful. The music, singing, acting, and the set designs were great. This opera was the best and most heart pounding performance I had ever seen. After the production, Ira Carol and I were invited to meet donors, musicians, and Anthony at a reception. Anthony introduced us to Artistic Director James Levine and other musicians. As we were socializing and talking to various people, a woman approached us and was introduced by Anthony. Stephanie C. Mortimore plays piccolo in the MET orchestra. This musician shocked Ira Carol and me when she said:

> I was at DePaul when Anthony first played for Larry Combs. I saw this small kid come out of a room I had passed by a few minutes earlier. I was surprised to see such a young clarinet player who played so beautifully.

Anthony was only eleven-years-old at the time.

In November of 2001, Mrs. Pfealzer visited Cincinnati to see and hear Anthony perform with his new orchestra, the Cincinnati Symphony. After the solo performance, Mrs. Pfealzer said, "He was there in his white tie and tails, and I just burst into tears. I was very proud."

Mrs. Pfealzer is no longer with us physically, but mentally and spiritually she will always be working her magic on all of us, especially the children. Anthony is currently a member of Merit School of Music's National Advisory Board.

This experience is another example of the importance of finding the best teachers for children. Bad teachers can destroy a child's enthusiasm and his ability to learn. Do whatever it takes to ensure that your children have the best teachers possible.

The Interlochen Center For The Arts is another amazing training ground for young artists. Interlochen, which is located in northwest Michigan on twelve hundred acres of scenic woodlands and situated between two beautiful glacial lakes, was founded in 1928 as this country's first music camp.

Today, Interlochen is comprised of a four and an eight-week summer camp for students aged eight through eighteen, the Arts Academy Boarding School for high school students, and a training program designed for adult learners was recently added.

During the summer months, over 2500 students come to Interlochen from all fifty states and fifty different countries. Some of the most talented youngsters in the world migrate to Interlochen during the summer to study music, visual arts, acting, dancing, writing, and motion picture arts. According to Interlochen's website, "10% of the personnel of the major symphony orchestras across the world are Interlochen Arts Camp alumni."

Each year, five hundred students attend the Interlochen Arts Academy Boarding School. This school is considered one of the top four-year arts high schools in the country. Anthony spent his last two years of high school at the Arts Academy. He studied clarinet with Mr. Richard Hawkins, who is currently Associate Professor of Clarinet at Oberlin Conservatory of Music.

Demarre and Anthony first attended the Interlochen Arts Camp after receiving partial scholarships from the Sherwood Conservatory of Music and the Merit Music Program, respectively. Ira Carol and I had to pay the three thousand dollar balance each summer. At the time, I felt that the cost of sending them to Interlochen was too high, but Ira Carol–as she always does–convinced me that the music training they would receive here was worth the cost. I relented, and today realize that the act of sending them to this music camp was one of several expensive, life-changing decisions we made, that lead to our sons becoming successful professional musicians.

Anthony spent his first summer at Interlochen in the Junior Division and the following year we enrolled him in the Intermediate Division. Demarre started in the Intermediate and advanced to the Senior Division the following year.

The summer of 1990 was a monumental time of major accomplishments for our sons. Both were winners in their respective division's concerto competition. For two young African American brothers to win such prestigious competitions was unheard of. Demarre was fifteen-years-old and Anthony was eleven. This experience caused both my sons to realize how immensely talented they were. Being named winners in the concerto competitions also made them realize they could compete with any young musician, no matter what race, ethnicity, gender, or social class.

Their concerto successes caused Demarre's and Anthony's enthusiasm for music, their positive attitude, and self-esteem, to soar to new heights. Although our sons' self-confidence was always high, after the concerto wins, Ira Carol and I saw distinct changes in their study habits. Demarre and Anthony knew they were talented, but as a result of their summer of 1990 accomplishments, they proved to themselves that their music making ability was exceptional. They came home possessed with the music bug. This was obvious to us because of the long hours they spent practicing. Their musical intelligence and passion for music, paved the way for them to become accomplished musicians, and more than anything, two self-confident mature teenagers.

# DEMARRE MCGILL

*Demarre at Interlochen Arts Camp.*

Winning the Interlochen concerto competition was one of the goals Demarre set for himself. The act of attaching his written goals to the wall of his bedroom motivated him every day. Anthony was also reading Demarre's goals, and at the age of eleven, he accomplished the same objective as his big brother. They fed off each other's successes then and continue to do so today. Along with their mother and me, the brothers are each other's loudest cheerleader. They never miss an opportunity to compliment each other.

Demarre's first summer at the Interlochen Arts Camp had a profound impact on him. The following is an excerpt from an article by Howard Reich, entertainment writer for the *Chicago Tribune.* Mr. Reich interviewed him for an article, which appeared in the newspaper on May 20, 1991.

There were all these really tough young players there (Interlochen Arts Camp) and I couldn't believe that I could play on their level—so that's when I realized that I really might have something here, McGill says.

So I came home and started practicing hours and hours, and my parents had to tell me to calm down and take it easy.

Expose children to positive experiences and good teachers, and without even knowing it, you just might be establishing a career path for that five, ten or fifteen-year-old.

During a *Chamber Music Society* interview, Demarre was asked: "When did you decide to become a professional musician and why?" Demarre responded:

This came about when I was fifteen-years-old at Interlochen Arts Camp in Michigan. That summer, I really liked a clarinetist, but she just wanted to be friends. I said 'OK,' but was still determined to change her mind. I was scheduled to play the Khachaturian Flute Concerto with the orchestra and had created a story about the concerto. In this story I am a knight, and she is the princess I have to save. I gave her this story as a gift, and promised to play every note for her. Playing that piece at the concert was the first time I really made music for someone. She liked it a lot (smile). Anyway, when I realized the endless possibilities of music making, I was hooked forever.

Anthony attended Whitney M. Young Academic Center for seventh and eighth grades. He graduated in June of 1993. The Academic Center is housed in the same building as Whitney Young Magnet High School, which proudly boasts that First Lady, Michelle

Obama, was an honors graduate. This school is still considered one of the best high schools in the City of Chicago. Anthony studied for one year at Whitney Young Magnet High School.

During Anthony's freshman year at Whitney Young High, Ira Carol and I noticed that on several occasions he returned home with torn clothing and scratches on his face and neck. We asked him to tell us what was going on, but he didn't provide much information. We knew he was involved in fights, but he would not tell us who he was fighting, or why. The final straw happened when she visited the school to pick up Anthony's grades. While walking down the school corridor behind Anthony, another student walked up to him and said, "You better watch your back man." After arriving home that evening, she told me what the other student had said. We discussed this incident in the privacy of our bedroom, and made the decision to find another school for Anthony.

Ira Carol visited the University of Chicago Laboratory School. Anthony was tested and was accepted. Before we agreed to send him to this school, Chicago Lab allowed Anthony and his mother to spend a day in various classrooms with the teachers and students. We talked about this experience after they returned home. Anthony was apprehensive about attending Lab. He told his mother that he did not like the social aspects of the school. She informed him that the social climate of a school was not the most important thing to consider. The tuition was over fifteen thousand dollars per year, and the administrators did not offer any scholarship assistance to us, so we decided not to enroll him here.

During spring break, Ira Carol, Anthony, and I drove to Interlochen, Michigan to visit the Interlochen Arts Academy. We met with a woman who worked in the school's admissions office, and spent about forty minutes listening to her describe the school and the academic program. After a few hours on the campus, Anthony's facial expressions told us that this was the place for him. His face reminded me of the expression Anthony had when he picked up a clarinet for the first time. During this meeting, Ira Carol and I asked many questions—including—"how much is the yearly tuition?" Finally, the admissions officer stated that the tuition was over $20,000 per year. We looked at her and then at each other, eyes wide open. This huge tuition fee shocked us.

We left her office and spent the next two hours admiring the natural beauty of the campus. We walked through all the buildings, occasionally stopping to listen to the student performances or practice sessions. Before leaving, we made the decision that this was the place where Anthony would finish his high school education. We would figure out how to round up the tuition money later.

Ira Carol and I submitted an application to the Academy and after sending transcripts and other documentation, we were notified of Anthony's acceptance. He was proud of himself and we were also proud of him. The annual tuition at this prestigious school seemed out of our reach, but we did not allow this to deter us from sending our son to this school. Anthony's excitement about the possibility of attending the Arts Academy was evident. We applied for and received about eight thousand dollars in scholarship assistance, and took out a second mortgage on our home to cover the balance of the tuition and fees.

Anthony excelled in all of his academic and music studies during his first year at the Interlochen Arts Academy–his sophomore year of high school. The following school year, he was just as successful. During the early spring of 1996, his junior year, Ira Carol and I sat down with Anthony to review his transcripts from Whitney Young High School and the Whitney Young Academic Center. We realized that based upon the high school credits Anthony received while in 7th and 8th grade at the Academic Center, he had taken enough courses to meet the Interlochen Arts Academy's graduation requirements after spending only two years there. We submitted a letter to the administrators requesting that he be allowed to graduate after his junior year.

We were told that they could not promise early graduation, but would review all of his records and inform us of their decision.

Shortly after Ira Carol and I started this process, we were notified that in June of this school year, Anthony would in fact have obtained all of the Academy's graduation requirements. We were elated. At age sixteen, Anthony graduated with honors from the Interlochen Arts Academy.

Now, the bigger question was; What college would he attend? Because Demarre was preparing to graduate from the Curtis Institute of Music, Anthony submitted an application and auditioned here. Our timing was perfect. He aced the audition and was accepted as a student to fill the only clarinet spot available. I signed the Curtis acceptance agreement on April 24, 1996.

Anthony spent four years at Curtis and graduated from this prestigious music school just as his big brother had. It gives me great joy when I think back on the roads my sons travelled to accomplish their goals, and how hard they worked in their quest to be the best.

At this time in their careers, Demarre and Anthony realized the power inherent in their music making. This shows that while parents are agonizing on how to ensure the safety and success of their child, the child is also planning for present and future successes. This is almost like saying, "two heads are better than one." You could also say that three heads (mom, dad, and child) are better than one. We can actually take this thought to another level and say that all the positive influences of the people in a child's life-immediate family, relatives, teachers, and friends—serve to shape and mold the child into a successful person.

Parents, use all the resources available to you to raise your child. No matter how high that child-raising mountain might seem, start climbing it with your child early in his life.

Interlochen continues to be a part of Anthony's musical life. On May 27, 2012, he was invited back to celebrate the Interlochen Arts Academy's 50th Anniversary. The Academy presented Anthony the 2012 Alumni Ovation Award for his accomplishments and contributions to the field of music.

Demarre and Anthony also spent summers at Marlboro Music, performing with some of the world's top classical musicians. Marlboro was founded in 1951 and is located in the small town of Marlboro, Vermont.

> Marlboro Music is acclaimed world-wide as an institution devoted to artistic excellence and to developing new musical leaders who illuminate all areas of music today. It is where the concept of having master artists play together with exceptional young professional musicians was born—initiating a...new approach to learning." *(www.marlboromusic.org)*

Marlboro Music was created to bring some of the most talented musicians together, "to share new perspectives and learn from one another, to inspire and be inspired." *(www.marlboromusic.org)*

At Marlboro, as it is affectionately called, Demarre and Anthony made beautiful music with, and learned from some of the most talented and well-known musicians of our time. One such musician was David Soyer, who was a founding member and cellist of the world-renowned Guarneri String Quartet. Mr. Soyer died on February 25, 2010 at the age of 87. On February 27, 2010, as a tribute to Mr. Soyer, Anthony wrote the following in his blog:

> When you get the opportunity to play with one of the great teachers, players and musicians of all time when

you are 18, it changes you. I became a 'professional' when I went to Marlboro Music Festival for the first time as an 18-year-old student because I learned that the only thing that was important was that I played music and took it very seriously. My early exposure to the Beethoven String Quartets was with the Guarneri Quartet recordings. Stunning. That first summer I got to play in a group with David Soyer and it was the Schubert Octet. The piece is like an hour long and it is one of the most beautiful pieces ever written. Getting to spend an hour on a stage with a great wise man is a gift in itself, but we rehearsed for hours and hours and also took the piece on tour, maybe playing 10 concerts or so. This is what I remember about the influence he had on me.

He was the foundation of the group. So solid and strong was how he played. These are also words that come to mind when I think of all those hours of rehearsal. Each phrase played with feet firmly planted on the ground, but with such freedom. Freedom to play as you wanted.

He would always talk about the fact that the person with the melody had the melody and that was it. When he would play a melody he owned it completely.

When he said something about music, you listened. The way he played a phrase you would think that was exactly the way it should be played. Such confidence and little doubt.

I learned to be strong and not mess around.

Being next to him on a stage you knew that this was serious business, not something to mess around with or toy with, but something extremely important. No funny business. Although as many people know, he was one of the funniest people I've ever met.

In rehearsals after much talking or debate, he would start playing almost immediately. This always seemed to say to everyone, Shut up!

This is what matters, the sounds, the music. His music lives and we can hear him now as before. We can hear him still every day, every second that we want to. He has given us so much and we have that forever.

Thank you for playing with me, for me, and teaching me with every note and every slide…

Thank you Mr. Soyer *(Anthony McGill's Blog 2-27-10)*

The positive influences good teachers have on children cannot be overstated. Always be aware of the fact that children will let you know whether their teachers are good for them or not. It is up to you as parents to talk to your child about his teachers, and listen to him during these conversations. On some occasions, you might have to find new teachers, or new schools. More likely than not, if you have done your homework, you will be reading positive stories about your child's teachers, such as the story Anthony told about Mr. David Soyer.

Raise your children by being a positive example for them to follow. Ira Carol and I were role models for Demarre and Anthony. If they see you studying, reading, writing, singing, painting, or preparing for that big exam, chances are they will do the same when they get older. If they see you fighting, cursing, using illegal drugs, or abusing legal ones, chances are they will follow your lead and before you know it, they are doing the same things.

Expose your children, support and compliment them. These are just three of the many keys to raising successful children. Expose them to as many cultural, artistic, athletic, and educational activities and programs as possible. Be careful of burnout. Balance outside activities by developing a list of ones your child has shown interest in, and periodically enroll him in one or two.

You might think that this journey is a long one. It is not. Before you know it, your child will be graduating from high school and college, and moving into that part of life we call adulthood.

And yes, compliment your children at every opportunity. That big hug, pat on the back, or the words, "good job," means a lot to them, whether you realize this or not.

*Fifteen-year-old Demarre preparing to perform the Khachaturian Flute Concerto with the Chicago Symphony Orchestra in 1991. Photo by Jim Steere © Chicago Symphony Orchestra Association.*

# CHAPTER ELEVEN

## AWARDS AND RECOGNITIONS

Demarre won many music competitions during his pre-teen and teenage years. Some of the major ones were: St. Paul Federal Bank Concerto Competition, the Interlochen Arts Camp Concerto Competition, General Motors & Seventeen Magazine National Concerto Competition, ACT-SO Competition, the Chicago Youth Symphony Orchestra Concerto Competition, and the National Flute Talk Magazine Concerto Competition.

One of the most prestigious was the Chicago Symphony Orchestra and Illinois Bell, Illinois Young Performers Competition that was broadcast live on WTTW-PBS Chicago, in May of 1991. He was fifteen-years-old at the time. The finalist performed solo with the orchestra. The competition winners were announced after the young musicians finished their performances.

This competition was held during the time when many male teenagers in the African American community wanted to wear Nike shoes, which cost a fortune compared to the six dollar Converse Allstar gym shoes I wore during the 60s.

My Allstars had soft canvas tops that covered the ankle, dark brown rubber soles, and the trademark Converse star stenciled on each shoe. Boys growing up during this period weren't cool unless they had a pair of Allstars, a couple pair of khaki pants, and some plaid shirts. Don't even think about coming into the gym without Allstars on your feet. If you had a pair on, other players might be deceived into believing you could actually play. I used this deception many times until I was exposed after being chosen to play on a three-on-three playground basketball team.

Although it seemed that I was always the shortest boy on the court, I was able to score a few points. The shoes actually made me feel taller than my five feet seven inch frame. Someone could have made a super-hero movie about my basketball exploits, especially the time I made that game-winning slam dunk over a seven-foot tall opponent... Yeah! I'm still dreaming. My self-confidence has always been high, but I definitely could not slam the ball over a seven footer.

Before the 1991 Chicago Symphony Orchestra competition concert, Demarre asked me, "Could you buy me a pair of Nikes." I told him that I would never spend one hundred dollars for a pair of gym shoes. "Shoes don't make the man," I said. Well, after he won the Chicago Symphony competition, I broke down and immediately after he performed with the symphony, instead of presenting him with a customary bouquet of flowers, I gave him a box containing a pair of those expensive Nike shoes. It was very funny watching Demarre walk around Orchestra Hall holding

*Demarre was "First Place Winner" in the 1988 St. Paul
Federal Bank's Junior Division concerto competition. Photo
courtesy of St. Paul Federal Bank For Savings.*

a Nike shoebox containing a pair of gym shoes. I even bought myself a pair. The shoes were comfortable and I still have mine. Demarre was elated. After leaving Orchestra Hall, he put the shoes on as soon as we got into our car. He really looked good in his black tuxedo and those Nike gym shoes. This would have been a great TV commercial for Nike. I can hear Demarre saying, "Just Do It." He won the prestigious competition, a $1,930 check, and a pair of expensive Nike gym shoes. He probably felt as tall as I did when in 1964 at the age of fourteen; I purchased my first pair of Converse Allstars. Thank God for paper routes. That job put a few dollars into my pockets and allowed me to buy those magical shoes.

In 1993, Anthony also competed in the Chicago Symphony Orchestra and Illinois Bell, Young Performer's competition. Ira Carol and I always accompanied our sons to all of their competitions. When we arrived at Orchestra Hall, a male African American security guard met us in the foyer. He asked, "Who are you here for?" I responded, "Anthony is a contestant in the Illinois Young Performers competition. He is here to compete in the Junior Division." We introduced ourselves and the guard remembered that Demarre won the competition in 1991. He looked at Anthony and said, "I know you're not as good as your brother." Demarre was standing next to me and seemed surprised by this comment. Without hesitation, Ira Carol said, *"No, he is better."* She did not say this as a means of comparing our sons with each other. She was shocked that this person would say what he did while Anthony and Demarre were standing there, three feet from him. Anthony was on his way to a competition involving some of the most talented young musicians in the Chicago area and did not need to hear this comparison. Such negative statements can have detrimental effects on children.

Our sons have always been supportive of each other. They had their normal childhood arguments and disagreements, but we never allowed them to fight or disrespect each other, nor did we allow others to make negative comments or comparisons about them. Ira Carol and I were always there and knew when to step in to mitigate these situations.

Adults must never compare siblings as the security guard did. After hearing the guard's statement, Ira Carol immediately went into damage control mode. Her response also served to provide positive reinforcement for Anthony. He performed beautifully and won an honorable mention in the competition.

We thought he would win the following year, but unfortunately, the greatest youth music competition in the State of Illinois and possibly the entire Midwest was discontinued several months later. The honorable mention award did not stunt Anthony's musical growth. He began to practice even more. He knew that he wanted to be the best, just like his brother, and nothing would stop him from accomplishing this goal.

Ten years after Demarre won the Chicago Symphony Orchestra competition, Anthony actually used the famous Nike phrase, "Just Do It." He used it to describe his motivation after playing a clarinet solo part with the Cincinnati Symphony Orchestra in January of 2001. Anthony won the Associate Principal Clarinet position in this orchestra in 2000, when he was twenty-years-old, and officially became a member of this orchestra after graduating from Curtis Institute of Music.

> I wasn't thinking about the weather or about anyone in the audience. When that clarinet goes into my mouth, I'm thinking about playing, Mr. McGill says. You know the Nike commercials–'Just Do It?' It's kind of like that. Athletes do it. It's the zone. It's the same thing with that solo. *(Cincinnati Enquirer, Janelle Gelfand, January 21, 2001)*

In 2010 and 2011, Anthony was honored by the African American news website *The Root,* as one of "The 100 most influential African Americans..."

"The 2010 Root 100 recognizes emerging and established African American leaders who are making extraordinary contributions. The Root 100 celebrates leadership, creativity, service and above all, excellence." Over the past three years, many of this country's greatest educators, politicians, journalist, artist, athletes, and business leaders have been honored by *The Root.* Corey Booker, Tyra Banks, Benjamin Todd Jealous, Beyoncé Knowles, John Legend, and Van Jones are just a few of the past honorees.

Anthony recently told us:

> Being honored as a member of *The Root 100,* along with so many other great African Americans, made me feel really, really good.

163

I told Anthony: "I am not surprised. Before your career is over you and your brother will receive many more honors. Your dedication, hard work, and your willingness to 'give back,' causes people to take notice and acknowledge you for who you are and what you do. Congratulations Anthony."

On March 15, 2012, Anthony received another great honor. Anthony, violinist Tai Murray, and violinist Elena Urioste were awarded the first annual, *Award of Excellence*, by The Sphinx Organization. Founded in 1996 by Aaron Dworkin and Carrie A. Chester, this organization was established, "to increase the participation of Blacks and Latinos in music school, as professional musicians, and as classical music audiences."

The awards ceremony was held in the building housing the *Temple of Justice*, commonly known as the Supreme Court of the United States. Supreme Court Justices Sonia Sotomayor, Ruth Bader Ginsberg, and Stephen Beyer introduced the winners and presented the awards to them. Several congressmen, heads of top music conservatories and schools, music organizations, and many top tier executives from the business community were also in attendance.

Ira Carol, Anthony's girlfriend Abby, and I were invited to attend. According to Mr. Dworkin, many of the 100 or so guests described the black tie dinner affair as being "perfect." I still do not know how the event organizers were able to put this elaborate program together "in one month." The interior of this huge building was beautiful. The entire building–exterior and interior– is constructed of marble. The carved marble busts of the former chief justices are artistic masterpieces. The hand rails following the marble stairs were carved from blocks of marble and did not extend outward from the walls but were a part of the marble blocks they were carved from.

Before dinner, guests were invited to attend a short lecture about the court. No photographs were allowed inside the court, but could be taken from the doorway. Anthony was super sharp in his tailor

*Photo of Justice Thurgood Marshall's portrait, which is displayed in the Supreme Court building. Courtesy of the artist, Mr. Simmie Knox.*

made black tuxedo. Justice Ginsburg introduced Anthony. After she presented the heavy medallion to him, they hugged affectionately. Justice Ginsburg's big smile showed that she was proud of him. After the program, Anthony said, "Justice Ginsburg loves opera."

While walking through the majestic halls, I looked up at some of the large oil portraits of past justices and saw a painting of the first African American Supreme Court Justice. I paused, thinking of the magnitude of the fact that Justice Thurgood Marshall became a member of this court on October 2, 1967. This was over forty-five years ago, during the heart of the civil rights movement.

While I was admiring the portrait of Justice Thurgood Marshall, I heard Ira Carol calling me, *"D, come here. Look at this. D, you need to take a picture of this."*

I didn't know what she was talking about, but I quickly photographed the portrait with my phone camera. I took a couple of pictures and turned the corner where Ira Carol and several of the other guests were leaning over a 4-foot high railing, straining to look upward. I approached the area, squeezed my wide body between two other people in this small space, looked up and marveled at this beautiful site. We were looking up at a magnificent spiral staircase. Although the building is only ninety-two feet tall, this staircase seemed to spiral endlessly, ending at an illuminated translucent pearl like dome.

The three honorees performed at different times during the program. Their music making was beautiful and the music bounced off the marble walls and ceiling with penetrating sharpness—creating an audio illusion of several musicians playing simultaneously. The guests—who seemed to be frozen—sat motionless as each musician played, and burst into loud cheering and applause after their performances.

On February 1, 2013, my sons were honored by *theGrio.com's 100: Making History Today.* TheGrio.com, a division of NBC, is a "video-centric news community site devoted to providing African Americans with stories and perspectives that appeal to them but are underrepresented in existing national news outlets." TheGrio's press release stated:

> Anthony McGill and Demarre McGill are brothers who although born and raised on Chicago's tough South Side, have both achieved stellar levels of success in the world of classical music...

As a result of theGrio's 100 honors, Demarre and Anthony were featured on NBC's Nightly News with Brian Williams, the TODAY Show, the Melissa Harris-Perry Show and The Steve Harvey Show.

*Anthony proudly wearing his Sphinx "Award of Excellence" medal.*

On many occasions during the past three decades, my sons have been recognized as great musicians and most importantly, great human beings. Because of their work ethic and their love of humanity, Demarre and Anthony will undoubtedly continue to be honored by individuals and organizations across the world.

*Fifteen-year-old Demarre after performing the Khachaturian Flute Concerto with the Chicago Symphony Orchestra in 1991. Photo by Jim Steere © Chicago Symphony Orchestra Association.*

# CHAPTER TWELVE

## MRS. LEVITIN, MR. JARRETT AND GOAL SETTING

M rs. Susan Levitin was one of Demarre's most influential early flute teachers. She is well-known in the Midwest as being one of the best teachers of young flute students. As an introduction to Demarre's performance on the Illinois Young Performers competition TV broadcast, Mrs. Levitin said:

Demarre is a very unusual teenager. He has his goals clearly set out and he has his priorities very much in order. He is able to do this and still be a normal teen-ager. The amazing thing is that he wakes up every morning, looks at what his goals are posted on the wall of his room, and then goes for them every day of his life.

When asked about the music Demarre played during the competition, Mrs. Levitin said:

It was just about a year ago this spring (1990) when Demarre came into a lesson and he said very shyly, 'Do you think I could work on the Khachaturian Concerto?' And I said, if that is what you would like to do and you feel that you would like to put in that kind of effort to learn a piece of that difficulty, fine. And then he said, 'Well I have it for you. I have it learned and memorized.' And he played the first movement of the Khachturian Concerto for me, which he had done completely on his own.

Demarre was also interviewed as part of the television production. He stated the following:

For me, it is important to have a strong sense of what I want because I become lazy once in a while, and whenever I look on my wall and see those goals, I realize that I can't stop now, so I always keep pushing. I have one overall goal and it is to be the best flutist in the world. I don't necessarily want to be famous, but I want to be the best. The best.

One important point to remember about this quote is that Demarre was fifteen-years-old. He knew what he wanted and with the help of his parents, teachers, friends and others, he developed a plan and implemented it successfully. He did not accomplish his early goals in a vacuum. We were there when he needed us.

This dedication to music and willingness to study and work hard to achieve his goals and objectives, even at this young age, is still being practiced by Demarre. At thirty-eight years of age, he is still setting goals and taking the necessary steps to achieve them.

Prior to the finals competition that was held in Chicago's Orchestra Hall, Mr. Howard Reich, entertainment writer for the *Chicago Tribune* interviewed Demarre for an article that appeared in the newspaper on May 20, 1991. The following is an excerpt from the article:

> Nervous? Are you kidding? I've been dreaming about this moment for three years...When I first watched the contest on TV three years ago, I thought to myself: I've got to get this—I've got to have it. Even though I've been planning on this, I still can't exactly believe I'm going to be playing with the CSO...The CSO is so great, I can hardly wait to meet its flutist, like [principal] Donald Peck, adds McGill, a flutist in the junior division. Now that I think about it, maybe I will be a little nervous. I don't know for sure that I'm going to become the best flutist in the world or even the best one on my block, McGill says. But I know I'll never get there if I don't keep aiming at it.

It is amazing that Demarre was twelve-years-old when he first envisioned himself winning this great competition. He set a high and difficult goal for himself. We supported and encouraged him, but he did the hard work and accomplished another one of his major objectives.

During a video interview for the Chicago Youth Symphony Orchestra in May of 2012, Demarre was asked, "Do you have any advice for young people?" He responded:

> It's a good idea to know what you are striving for. It's easy to get lost. What do you want to do? I find it very useful and helpful to be very specific.

I want to go to this college. I want to be better than this person because this person is amazing...you'll find yourself accomplishing those goals
if you know exactly what those goals are. *(CYSO
website)*

Ira Carol and I recently watched the video of Demarre
winning the Illinois Young Performance Competition. While
sitting on our sofa and watching on a large flat screen TV connected to a surround sound speaker system, I had flashbacks
of the actual performance. Orchestra Hall was filled to its
capacity with people. We felt the excitement of everyone in
attendance. The buzz in the hall and foyer was loud before the
start of the program and many of the attendees were friends,
acquaintances, or other people we met at competitions or
music schools. It seemed like everyone in the hall was standing
and talking to someone else. Ira Carol, Anthony, and I were
nervous, but we never allowed the huge smiles to disappear
from our faces.

As usual, my heart was pounding and my hands were
sweaty. Ira Carol would occasionally grab my right hand
and squeeze it while we stared into each other's eyes. When
Demarre finished his performance, we, along with everyone
else in the audience, jumped to our feet and screamed as
loud as we could. Later, when he was introduced as one of the
winners, tears started flowing down Ira Carol's face. I hugged
Anthony, and Ira Carol put her arms around both of us. *"He
did it,"* she screamed. I tried to maintain my composure by
only saying, "WOW." I do believe we were more nervous than
Demarre. I'm sure he had flashbacks to that day when he
was twelve-years-old and dreaming about winning this major
competition.

*Flutist Susan Levitin and her husband David.*
*Photo courtesy of Susan Levitin.*

This proves that goal setting needs to start early in a child's life-the earlier the better.

After Demarre won this huge competition, Mr. Vernon Jarrett, a columnist with the *Chicago Sun-Times*, wrote the following in his weekly column:

> Congratulations to Mr. Michael Jordan. He deserves every accolade he's received as the 1991 Most Valuable Player of the National Basketball Association. But what about Demarre L. McGill?
>
> When you scan a photo of the youthful McGill, you can easily visualize a 15-year-old Jordan. The big

difference is that McGill at 15 is far more advanced as a flautist than was Jordan as a basketball player at the same age. But they share a willingness to become truly good at what they wanted to do.

Well, I can tell you that there are other Demarre L. McGills in the black community, not to mention the potential ones who can do with flutes, pianos, horns, test tubes, beakers and words what Michael Jordan does with a basketball. What they need is a little encouragement to learn and practice, practice, practice–just like Demarre and Michael. *(Chicago Sun-Times May 23, 1991)*

Mr. Jarrett was correct when he said there are many other super talented teenagers in the African American community. It is unfortunate that the world does not acknowledge most of these children. The media devotes much of its news stories on the negative images of shootings, other crimes, fighting politicians, and little coverage of the positive things happening in communities across America.

Violence in neighborhoods across this country seems to be at epidemic levels, but there should be balance in how the news is covered. The Demarres, Anthonys, and all the other successful young African American children in small and large cities across this country, should be written about, talked about, and shown in the media. These positive images of our youth could go a long way to motivate other youngsters in our neighborhoods, and inspire them to want to be great.

Mr. Vernon Jarrett, who died on May 23, 2004, also worked for the Chicago Defender Newspaper and was a member of the editorial boards of the Chicago Tribune and the Chicago Sun-Times. He was the founder of the NAACP's Afro-Academic, Cultural, Technological and Scientific Olympics (ACT-SO). ACT-SO is a national competition that showcases and provides scholarships to young African American students. Mr. Jarrett, a great African American leader,

*Mr. Vernon Jarrett and me after Demarre's and Anthony's*
*south side recital. McGill family photo.*

understood the need for parents and the community at large to
encourage and help our youth be the best that they can be.

He motivated thousands of young students, and to this day,
ACT-SO continues to support children across America. The
determination and drive to be the best has to start early in a
child's life.

Although there are many community organizations, which provide
positive services to children, parents should be the primary teachers
and motivators, and should try to instill these attributes in their young
children. This guidance could simply be helping the children with
their homework or science fair project, and insisting that the work is
completed. Just be there for and with your children. Help them when
they need help and provide encouragement when necessary.

The following are the goals Demarre wrote on a sheet of notebook paper, and then on a poster board that he taped to a wall in his bedroom when he was fourteen-years-old:

## GOALS FOR THE SUMMER 1990

Win Interlochen Concerto Competition-Interlochen Arts Camp
Be 1st in Concert Orchestra-Interlochen Arts Camp
Get into World Youth Symphony Orchestra-Interlochen Arts Camp

## GOALS FOR THE SCHOOL YEAR

Never make another mistake in practicing or performing
To get all A's and B's on my report card
To be rated the best young flautist in the state
Win Illinois Young Performers
Win Chicago Youth Symphony Concerto Competition

## GOALS FOR THE FUTURE

To be the best flautist in the world

Demarre accomplished most of the early goals that he established for himself. Well, almost all of them. I'm not so sure he was able to practice without making a mistake, although he is still striving for that perfection. His desire to be the best flutist in the world is still foremost in his mind, and he is still searching for that perfect practice session.

Parents should constantly talk to their children about the importance of establishing goals. Make sure your children write down their goals and post them on the bedroom door, on the wall, or in any conspicuous place where the entire family can see them

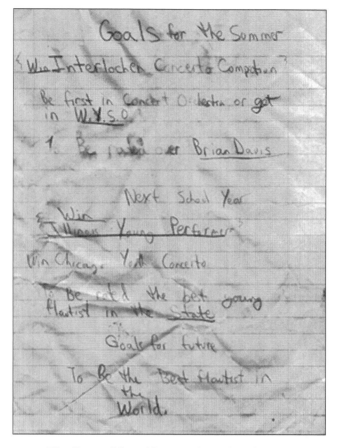

*The first writing of Demarre's goals written on
a sheet of notebook paper in 1990.*

every day. Tell them that it is normal for their goals to change over time and that it is also normal to have more than one goal. Find a way to reward them when they reach their goals. For those goals that your child is having a difficult time accomplishing, give him more assistance and encouragement.

Anthony also set high goals for himself when he was a child, and accomplished many of them as he watched and was influenced by his big brother's successes.

He pushed me a lot to work really hard–to practice and just inspired me without talking–by just picking up his flute constantly and practicing, before I played the clarinet. *(Anthony McGill, Chicago Youth Symphony Orchestra website)*

Anthony saw his brother's goals taped to the wall of his bedroom and today he is still setting goals for himself. In a January 20, 2009 article in the Chicago Tribune newspaper, Anthony said:

As Obama says he did, I tried to just work hard when I was the only black person in the room; that's the important thing. It wasn't any odd–man out type of focus. You've got to have your eye on the goal, not on your idea of a barrier.

Establishing well-defined goals is important for adults and is equally important for young children. A child's goals could be as simple as keeping the clothes off the bedroom floor, making the honor roll in school, being a starter on the high school basketball team, or being the President of the United States of America.

As the child becomes older, the goals will change and become more complex. Parents, always provide support, encouragement, and motivate your child to work hard in his quest to accomplish the goals.

Simeon Career Academy is a high school located on the South Side of Chicago, not far from our home. After the Simeon basketball team won another championship, Principal, Dr. Sheldon House, told students what the team accomplished is an example of what they should strive for in life. Dr. House said the team went through its ups and downs during the season, but persevered through their struggles to reach a team goal.

This is a great life lesson for our students, he told the *Chicago Crusader Newspaper*. Many of our students face challenges and obstacles at home and in their communities that can be overwhelming. But if they pick a goal, focus on it and get through the tough times, there is nothing they can't accomplish. *(Dr. Sheldon House, The Chicago Crusader, March 27, 2010)*

I was proud of the student athletes at Simeon when I heard the news they had won the State 4A basketball championship. Over the years, there have been some outstanding and talented Simeon students whose lives were cut short because of gun violence. But the Simeon administrators, teachers, and students, continue to reach many of the goals they set for themselves.

Goal setting is a crucial part of this success. As Dr. House said, if the students establish well-defined goals, "there is nothing they can't accomplish."

In his attempt to seek funding to help him pay for a new flute, on November 26, 1990, Demarre wrote and sent a letter to the New York Philharmonic, Music Assistance Fund. The following is the last paragraph of his letter:

My third and final goal is to be the best at whatever I do. I believe that the training and experience that I am getting at my age (15), will really prepare me for the competition that lies in the near future. Even if I don't accomplish all of my goals, I will always have music. Please consider me for a scholarship so that I can continue on my quest to reach these goals.

Demarre was not successful in this request, but he did not allow it to deter his quest to be the "best flautist in the world."

# Chapter Thirteen

## Philadelphia here we Come

B ecause Demarre was able to take several high school courses when he was in seventh and eighth grade at Kenwood Academic Center in Chicago, he was able to graduate after his junior year at Kenwood Academy High School, located in the Hyde Park-University of Chicago community on the South Side of Chicago, not far from where President Barack Obama's home is located. Although the Academy was considered one of the top high schools in the city during this time, Demarre was disillusioned about this school. He no longer wanted to attend. The prior year, a student was shot outside of the school and this upset him. During his junior year, I discussed the possibility of Demarre attending the University of Chicago. This world-class institution provided six full scholarships to children of Chicago Fire Department employees. I wanted him to tell me to submit an application for one of the scholarships. The positive influence on our finances would have been substantial if he received one of the six.

Demarre knew that he wanted to attend a top music school to prepare for a career as a professional musician. He looked at me, and in a deep voice, said, "No way." I asked him, "Why don't you want to go to the University of Chicago?" He responded, "The music school there is not where I want to study." I continued my attempt to convince him to allow me to submit an application for the U. of C. scholarship, but Demarre again said, "No way." I finally realized that he did not want to study music at the University of Chicago. I dropped the subject.

Ira Carol and I valued Demarre's opinion of where he wanted to continue his education. After the University of Chicago conversation, we asked him, "What school do you want to go to?" This is a prime example of how important it is for parents to listen to their children and allow them to participate in the decision-making processes that affect their lives.

Demarre presented Ira Carol and me with a list of five schools where he wanted to audition. Curtis Institute of Music in Philadelphia was number one on his list. The Juilliard School in New York was number two. The Peabody Institute in Baltimore, Oberlin Conservatory of Music located in Ohio, and Northwestern University's Bienen School of Music, in Evanston, Illinois, were the other three schools. We visited Oberlin Conservatory and Juilliard to talk to other students and teachers, and to get a *feel* for the schools. Demarre also visited Curtis Institute of Music.

While a student at the Interlochen Arts Camp, Demarre was told about Curtis Institute of Music. Mrs. Jeannette Kreston, Executive

Director of the Chicago Youth Symphony Orchestra, also gave him information about Curtis. Demarre was Principal Flutist and the first African American musician to win CYSO's concerto competition. Jeannette's daughters attended this famous school where many of the greatest musicians of our time studied. The Chicago Youth Symphony is considered one of the top youth orchestras in the United States. Over one hundred former members of CYSO are currently playing in professional orchestras around the world, or teaching at major music schools.

The following statement shows Demarre's sincere appreciation of the training he received while a member of this youth symphony:

> I really credit the CYSO for making me the musician I am today, because the level was so high. The flutists in the section were so amazing that I couldn't help but get better, and I'm forever grateful for that. *(Chicago Youth Symphony Orchestra website)*

During this time, Jeannette's daughter, Anthea, was attending Curtis. Jeannette suggested that we call Curtis and try to arrange a lesson with the flute teachers there. Mrs. Susan Levitin made a telephone call to Curtis and spoke to Mr. Jeffrey Khaner, one of the two flute teachers. Although it wasn't clear if there was going to be a flute audition that year, Mr. Khaner agreed to provide one lesson with Demarre and a date was set.

Ira Carol and I were initially apprehensive about sending Demarre to Philadelphia. We could not accompany him and knew that if he were going to have the lesson, he would have to go to Philadelphia by himself. He was sixteen-years-old, and we thought too young to go to the East Coast unaccompanied. Ira Carol and I asked him how he felt about traveling to Philadelphia alone. Without hesitation he said, "I'll be okay. I can take care of myself."

Again, his self-confidence trumped our apprehension. After much soul searching, we finally decided to allow him to go.

The Kreston family helped us with this decision. During his visit to Philadelphia, he stayed with Jeannette's daughter. I recently asked Demarre if he was afraid during his first trip to Philadelphia. Demarre answered, "No, I wasn't afraid. I was mostly intrigued by this dark, gritty, grungy city."

*After his Philadelphia audition, my husband and I started to receive telephone calls from some of the schools he was interested in attending. Mr. Julius Baker, a world-renowned flutist and teacher at Curtis called first. Mr. Khaner had told his colleague about the lesson he had with our son. The conversation was brief.*

Hello, Hello, may I speak with Mr. or Mrs. McGill?
*This is Mrs. McGill, who's calling?*
My name is Julius Baker, a flute teacher at Curtis. I heard how wonderful a flute player your son is and was wondering what your plans are for Demarre after high school?

*This conversation was one of several I had with Mr. Baker. A couple of months later, we received a call from Curtis informing us that an audition was scheduled for one flute position at the school. I informed Mr. Baker that Demarre's goal was to attend one of the top music schools, and that Curtis was number one on his list.*

I called Curtis and asked about the possibility of visiting the campus. The person I spoke to informed me that Curtis did not have a campus. Each year throughout its rich history, no more than 175 students attend this school, which is housed in an old grey stone mansion. Mary Louise Bok, who later became Mrs. Efrem Zimbalist, founded Curtis Institute of Music in 1924. The chartered purpose of this school was to "Train exceptionally gifted young musicians for careers as performing artists on the highest professional level." I was puzzled when told there was no campus, but we asked for and received an admissions application. Several weeks later, Demarre received an audition date. He immediately began to prepare for this audition. His practicing was intense and sometimes continued for hours on end. On many occasions we had to tell him to put the flute down and go to bed. At age sixteen, he knew what he wanted and his focus and determination showed us that he was ready for new musical challenges.

On a cold winter day in 1992, Demarre and I loaded our bags and his flute into my car and we headed toward Philadelphia. It was time for another long road trip related to Demarre's musical pursuits. I didn't know what to expect, but I had confidence in my son's ability to win the audition. Demarre kept telling me, "There is only one flute opening at the school." Talented young musicians from all over the world would be vying for this position. It seemed as though he was preparing me for the possibility of not having a successful audition. I tried my best to hide my nervousness.

When we were about two hundred miles west of Philadelphia, Ira Carol called me with some interesting news. Someone from the admissions office at The Juilliard School in New York called to inform Demarre he had been offered a scholarship. Here's how Ira Carol remembers it:

*This offering came as a great surprise to me, especially considering what had occurred several months before this call from Juilliard. My husband and I had taken Demarre to a college fair hosted by the Chicago Youth Symphony Orchestra. We spoke to a representative from Juilliard and asked about their Pre-College Program. The woman indicated that she felt it would not be a good idea to send Demarre to New York. She stated that males enrolled in the program did not do as well as females. She also said, 'They'll eat him alive.' She brought up so many negatives that we dismissed the idea of Demarre attending Juilliard's Pre-College Program.*

*Flutist James Galway also suggested that we not send Demarre to New York at such a young age. Demarre met Galway in 1989. He was in Chicago performing 'The Pied Piper Fantasy' with the Chicago Symphony Orchestra. Demarre and Anthony were members of the children's cast. While leaving a rehearsal, Demarre was walking southbound on Michigan Avenue about a block from Orchestra Hall. He saw Galway walking toward him. As they passed each other, Demarre, in a not so audible voice said, 'James Galway.' Galway heard him, turned around, introduced himself and invited Demarre to lunch. Demarre was smiling about this encounter days later. We saw James Galway after the performance and talked about Juilliard and New York.*

Demarre and I arrived in Philadelphia after driving about thirteen or fourteen hours. The flat highway that cut through Indiana was smooth as silk compared to the mountainous stretch of highway winding its way through the state of Pennsylvania. I love to drive, although driving through mountains is stressful to me. The mountaintop forest was beautiful, but I kept telling myself, "Keep your eyes the road."

After arriving in downtown Philadelphia, we checked into the Barclay Hotel next door to the school. The white translucent steam floating upward from street and sidewalk grates covering underground caverns was eerie. This hotel was old and dark. I could feel the ghosts of the thousands and thousands of people who once slept in this building. I imagined that some of the greatest musicians of the twentieth century stayed here while studying, teaching, or performing at Curtis Institute or at the Academy of Music in downtown Philadelphia.

The audition was the following day. We toured the school, ate dinner, and crashed out on the old-fashioned bed. We were exhausted. Although I was tired from the long drive, I was only able to sleep for about four or five hours. My nervousness seemed much greater than Demarre's. The stress I was experiencing reminded me of the physical pains I felt each time I attended my sons' recitals.

*Flutist James Galway, Katherine Naftzger, and Demarre after the Chicago Symphony Orchestra's Pied Piper Fantasy on April 25, 1989.*

The next day, Demarre took the audition and was told the results would be announced later on that same day. I told him that we could not wait for the results because a major winter snowstorm was brewing in the mountains just outside Philadelphia, and I had to return to work. He was disappointed we had to leave.

Forty-five minutes after we left and after entering the mountainous area of Pennsylvania, the storm hit us. The conditions were blizzard like. Visibility was low. The strong wind blowing the large snowflakes made my car's windshield wipers work overtime. The big trucks were traveling at least forty miles per hour and we were afraid because I could manage only about twenty-five, or thirty and sometimes slower. I was afraid to go faster. For safety reasons I refused to stop along the highway. Most of the rest areas were

*Flutist James Galway signing Anthony's program booklet.*

packed with big trucks and little cars, but we finally found one where we parked and rested a while. After calling Ira Carol on one of the pay phones, which I had to wait in line for about twenty minutes to use, we hit the road again. The snow continued to fall for the entire seventeen-hour trip home, although the weather became milder the closer we got to Chicago. I don't remember talking to my son much during our trip home. We seemed to be in a weird trance-like state of mind. The weather, the dangerous driving conditions, and the fact that we did not know the results of the audition kept our minds working overtime.

Demarre was probably angry with me for not waiting for the audition results. I tried my best to think positive about the audition, and I knew that throughout our sons' lives, Ira Carol and I drilled into their consciousness the importance of hard work and positive thinking. Being a human being however, negative thoughts occasionally crept into my mind, but the positive ones immediately wiped them out. I knew how hard Demarre had worked and how talented he was. The positive thoughts prevented me from agonizing about the possibility that he would not win the Curtis audition.

We were happy to see the flat earth of Indiana, even though every five miles or so, there were big trucks and cars rolled over in the ditches. The crosswinds blowing across this highway were difficult to handle. I never liked driving on this road, especially during winter.

Being a firefighter, I wondered about the people in those vehicles. Did they survive the accidents? Were the occupants still in their vehicles? I could not answer these questions and felt bad that I could not stop to help the victims. I prayed for them and kept on pushing up I-65 North. As soon as we arrived home, the exhaustion buckled my knees. The callous soles of my feet felt as though a million needles were penetrating to the bone. I don't remember what Demarre did after we made it home, but I immediately fell, fully clothed, unto my bed. My mind was racing like those big trucks, going too fast and splashing wet snow in all directions.

Five minutes later the telephone rang. I answered, "Hello." To my disbelief, it was an official from the Curtis Institute of Music calling to inform Demarre that he had been accepted into the Bachelor of Music program on a full scholarship. I was overjoyed and was no longer tired. I ran downstairs as fast as I could and found Demarre in the basement. I screamed, "That was a lady from Curtis. You did it. You're going to The Curtis Institute of Music." Demarre didn't say much, but his facial expression showed me how excited he was. We hugged each other and smiled all day long.

Demarre had been accepted into one of the top music schools. When Ira Carol returned home, she screamed after being told the good news. Demarre's first choice was now a reality. He scratched the remaining schools from his list. Demarre had accomplished another one of his goals. He was now a student at one of the most prestigious schools in the world.

For the first time in his young life, he would be living on his own–in his own apartment. This one bedroom unit was small, but after we decorated it, the space seemed to come alive and actually looked larger. The view was nothing to brag about, but Demarre did not seem to care. He just knew that at age seventeen, he had his own place within walking distance of Curtis Institute of Music. Shortly after being accepted into Curtis, Demarre said to his mother, "I'm so glad you and daddy were the kind of parents you were."

Ira Carol and I visited Philadelphia every chance we got. We spent many hours walking around downtown, dodging the ghostly steam, eating at one of the many restaurants, or just sitting on one of the benches in Rittenhouse Square Park.

This small park was a few hundred feet from the school, and was beautiful during the spring and summer months when the colorful flowers bloomed, and the different shades of green dominated the tree leaves. The park was shaped like a square and had diagonal sidewalks streaking through it like narrow airport runways. Together with the people walking through or relaxing on the benches, dogs, squirrels, and birds also strolled through it. We designated this area as our meeting place and spent many hours in this park.

During our warm weather visits to Philadelphia, Demarre met us here everyday. We talked, laughed, and eventually decided where we were going to eat our next meal. On many occasions we ate at Chicago's own Pizzeria Uno, located directly across the street from Curtis Institute.

*Ira Carol's mother, Eccorena Lake in Rittenhouse Square Park – 1996.*

After graduating from Curtis four years after he enrolled, Demarre did attend the Juilliard School in New York, where in 1998 he received his Master of Music Degree.

*Demarre, Anthony, and me in Demarre's Philadelphia apartment. Anthony moved here in 1996 after his brother moved to New York to pursue his Master's Degree at Juilliard.*

# CHAPTER FOURTEEN

## DON'T BE SURPRISED AND DON'T FEAR SUCCESS

Anthony received his Bachelor of Music degree from Curtis Institute of Music in 2000, and has performed throughout the United States, Europe and Asia. He has performed internationally in England, Poland, Germany, France, Lithuania, Spain, Czech Republic, Austria, Italy, Denmark, Switzerland, The Netherlands, Canada, Puerto Rico, South Africa and Japan.

At age twenty, while still a student at Curtis Institute of Music, he won the Associate Principal Clarinet job with the Cincinnati Symphony Orchestra, beating out 80 clarinetists from across the world that auditioned for the position. Many of the top clarinetist believed this was the best orchestra job available at the time. The fact that Anthony won this audition did not surprise us. We knew that he was a super talented musician who was motivated by seeing his brother practice five or six hours a day when he was a high school student.

Today, Anthony is the Principal Clarinetist of the Metropolitan Opera Orchestra in New York City. He has performed with the world's top chamber groups, including the Guarneri, Tokyo, Shanghai, Pacifica, Miro, Miami, Daedalus, and the Avalon String quartets, the Peabody Trio, the Poulenc Trio, and the Chicago Clarinet Ensemble. Anthony is currently on the faculty of the Juilliard School, John Hopkins University's Peabody Institute of Music, Mannes College, and the Bard College Conservatory. He has collaborated with musicians and artists such as the Brentano String Quartet, Musicians From Malboro, The Chamber Music Society of Lincoln Center, Mitsuko Uchido, Marina Piccinini and Barbara Sukova. Anthony has also performed with Yo-Yo Ma, Itzak Perlman, Gabriela Montero, Midori, Lang Lang, Yefim Bronfman, Gil Shaham and Emanuel Ax.

This is another example of one of a child's early activities becoming his profession with the child and the parents planning for it. Raising successful children does not happen by accident. It takes the hard work and dedication of fathers, mothers, other relatives, teachers, the extended family, and the children.

The audition process for orchestra jobs is extremely competitive and Anthony said that he, "could not believe it," when he won the MET Orchestra Principal Clarinet position. "I couldn't stand up. I had to sit down," was Anthony's response after the announcement.

Robert Fitzpatrick, Dean of the Curtis Institute of Music, in a 2001 article in the *Cincinnati Enquirer* said, "For a clarinetist to get a position right out of school of the quality he got is extremely rare.

Frankly, good clarinetists are a dime a dozen, so it takes something to rise above the crowd." In the same article, New York French hornist David Jolley said, "He has a rare package of tremendous playing skills and great ears–and then, a wonderful way with people."

Ira Carol and I truly believe that we gave Demarre and Anthony that extra "something," which helped them develop that "rare package." We define "something" as being life, love, support, encouragement, and a positive mental attitude to believe that they could achieve any goal they set for themselves. We also attempted to find the best teachers available to teach them outside of our home. These are very important principles parents must use to raise successful children. There are many more principles available. Find and use them daily.

Parents do not raise children in a vacuum. No matter how much love and support we gave our sons, we realized that other people outside of our home helped to raise our children. This is why parents must choose their children's schools and teachers carefully.

Get to know all of your child's teachers. Visit with them at school, or wherever the classes are being taught. Ira Carol and I attended our sons' parent and teacher meetings as often as possible. It is not a bad idea for you to accompany your child on class field trips. Teachers always need parental help on such excursions. Your child might not like this idea, but it serves a valuable purpose, and he will eventually get accustomed to seeing mom or dad on field trips, or in his classroom. The following is a quote from an editorial, which appeared in the *Chicago Sun-Times* on February 13, 2001:

> It is no surprise that researchers have found that schools tend to have fewer discipline problems when parents are involved.

Parents should be involved in every aspect of their children's lives. Begin to teach from the day they are born and don't stop. For your sons and daughters to be successful, you must be there, guiding them through the maze of life and the challenges, which lay before them. Exposure and support are two keys to this success. I will take this a step further and say that by finding and utilizing the right keys at the appropriate times, parents can unlock the positive creativity and genius that lives within all children. My wife and I raised our children to be successful men. We were not surprised when at age six; Demarre said he wanted to be a man when he grew up. Ira Carol and I were not surprised when he won the Florida Orchestra, San Diego Symphony, Seattle Symphony, and the Dallas Symphony principal flute positions, and would not have been surprised if he had been successful in the other auditions he took.

We were not surprised when Anthony won the Cincinnati Symphony Orchestra and the Metropolitan Opera Orchestra principal clarinet positions. We would not have been surprised if at age six, Anthony would have also said he wanted to be a man when he grew up, for he grew up to be a successful young man who has reached musical heights rare for someone his age. Don't be surprised when your child sets high goals, and don't be surprised when he reaches or exceeds them. With your help and guidance, your child can accomplish any task or reach any goal he sets. Anything is possible if you are there to guide him along the way.

*When our phone rang at about 8:00 P.M. on Wednesday, December 10th, my husband answered. The look on his face was confusing to me. The television volume was loud and he moved to another room in the house really fast. I followed him and searched his face in hopes of finding out what was going on. He gave me a thumbs up sign. I then knew that he was talking to Anthony. I felt like a little girl, 'let me talk, let me talk' I screamed excitedly. When my husband did not give me the phone, I ran upstairs and grabbed another one. I could hear Anthony's voice, but truly can't remember what was being said. I just knew he had won the Metropolitan Opera job! At age twenty-four, Anthony had reached another milestone. My baby had won the most prestigious clarinet position in the classical music world at the time! Ira Carol*

*Anthony and Demarre after Anthony won the Metropolitan Opera Orchestra Principal Clarinet position.*

Demarre was in New York on the day Anthony won the MET job. Ira Carol and I talked to both our sons on this night. There were moments when it seemed that all of us were once again screaming into the telephones at the same time. We finally calmed down and had a normal conversation about Anthony's major accomplishment. Anthony and his brother celebrated for hours on this night. I don't think they actually got any sleep until the next day. Anthony sent us photos of them smiling and hugging. The sincere joyous smiles on their faces showed us how happy they were, and that they are proud of each other's accomplishments.

*It has been two days since I heard the glorified news that Anthony won the principal chair position with the New York Metropolitan Opera Orchestra. Hearing this news caused me to open my computer and write my thoughts down. Why did it take me two days to do this? I guess it was my reaction of wonderment, excitement and apprehension. A strange combination of words, but my mind experienced all three of them. The first morning after I heard the news, I picked up my bible. It was around 3:30 A.M. when I allowed fear, or let's say a negative thought to enter my mind. I had to pray because I am generally a positive person.*

*My insecurities about Anthony's success, and the fear that someone or something would take it away from him caused my negative feelings. I needed to pray that God would protect my son and continue to surround him with goodness.*

*Anthony and his brother Demarre have always been very positive, confident, persistent, and hard workers. These are qualities that we instilled in them at a very young age. I am so proud of and deeply love both my sons. Both of them are moving into unchartered waters that neither I, nor their dad can go. This is both frightening and exhilarating, but as they have matured into outstanding, strong, and successful young men, I have come to a point that my fears have subsided. Ira Carol*

Ira Carol has gotten over her fears. She understands that her sons' mental fortitude and physical strength will see them through any obstacles thrown in front of them. We told our sons to always break through obstacles instead of going around them. The foundation we built for Demarre and Anthony can never be breached. Build a solid foundation for your children and they will, throughout their lives, construct houses that will never be blown down. Contrary to what we see on the nightly news, read in the newspapers, or on the Internet, I believe the majority of African American males in this country are positive hard working kids and adults. We just don't read about the positive contributions to society they are making. Unfortunately, the local and national news media tends to focus on the young males and females who are the violent troublemakers.

It is no accident that our sons are two of the many African American young males who are making positive contributions in their communities, and "doing the right things." We raised them the right way. Ira Carol and I provided them with the affection, support, and guidance necessary for them to develop the positive self-esteem children so desperately need to meet the tremendous challenges they face.

*Demarre, Ira Carol, and Anthony after her solo cabaret show on April 29, 2012.*

Accidents happen by accident. Raising successful, intelligent, responsible, talented, and positive young African American children does not happen by accident. It takes the efforts of parents, relatives, friends, and other members of the extended family. Some say, "It takes a whole village."

Parents must realize that they can't raise their children alone, and there is no magic formula for raising successful children. It is hard work. You must expose them to a wide variety of activities, which hopefully, are fun for the children and good learning experiences. The outside activities my wife and I chose were ones, which allowed Demarre and Anthony to exercise their minds and bodies. Music was just one of the activities they were involved in.

We did not sit down and draft a plan for developing two classical musicians, even though we knew that some of the world's greatest musicians started taking formal lessons when they were as young as three or four years old. We did however; want to involve them in as many activities as possible. This meant that we had to be the busiest non-paid chauffeurs in Chicago. Actually, we were being paid the highest salary any parent could possibly imagine, the fruits of which continue to grow right before our eyes. Our ultimate goal was to be the best parents we could possibly be, no matter what the cost. We had no idea that the price tag would be in the tens of thousands of dollars.

It is no secret that from the day they are born, in order for them to thrive mentally and physically, children have basic needs that must be met. Scientific research and past practices have proven that during the early stages of an infant's life, if he is not touched, or neglected physically and mentally, he may die. Researchers call this phenomenon "failure to thrive."

The following is a recent example of how important it is for parents to hug their infants and children:

> Kate and David Ogg cannot believe their 'miracle baby' was declared dead by doctors moments after he was born. Born at 27 weeks and weighing only 2 lbs., doctors battled for 20 minutes to save twin Jamie's life before giving his parents the devastating news he was dead, and placing him on his mother's bare chest so she could say goodbye.
>
> After five minutes of cuddling, stroking, and talking to her son, telling him she loved him, and that his twin sister Emily was OK, the Oggs were totally shocked when a miracle happened–Jamie came back to life.
>
> Despite being assured by doctors it was a natural reflex rather than signs of life, the Oggs persevered and two hours later, Jamie had opened his eyes, was moving

around and even drank some milk from his mother's finger. *(Rachel Quigley, dailymail.co.uk, 3-8-12)*

Ira Carol and I understood the importance of hugging our children every day. Be there with your child. Give him a big hug. Show and tell him how much you love him, even if he has trampled on that last nerve of yours. If he is not loved, he will not be capable of giving love. If he is not taught, he will not learn the positive attributes you hope to see in your child. Your son's life depends on you. Show him some love; it might just save his life.

Ira Carol and I spent a tremendous amount of time with our sons. Picnicking in the park, playing basketball in the backyard, going to the movies, playing board games at home, and reading to them, were just a few of the time consuming activities which helped to mold Demarre and Anthony into the positive and successful young men they are today. Driving them to karate, art, tennis, swimming, gymnastics, basketball, and music classes, and attending all of their performances, was a normal routine for Ira Carol and me. These activities helped them develop a strong and positive self-esteem. Their self-confidence soared during these very active times.

The following are quotes by Demarre and writer Kurt Loft that appeared in the *Tampa Tribune* on January 12, 2003:

Demarre McGill won't take all the credit for landing a job as principal flutist with the Florida Orchestra. Nor will he give himself a pat on the back for his virtuosic gifts as a classical musician. He praises his parents.

We're the ones who are proud of them, says McGill, whose younger brother, Anthony, is also a musician. They supported us, and they get the credit. They're a huge part of who I am and the way I think. And I appreciate them because I know how difficult it is to raise children.

They instilled in us a positive mental attitude. We were never allowed to say can't.

According to Kurt Loft, "The brothers fed off each other's enthusiasm and the support of their parents."

## *THE MIND*

*The mind is miraculous*
*It can process and store information*
*The mind never rests and it's yours*
*It will create for you, destroy, and even die for you*
*The mind is powerful*
*It can take you places you have never been*
*It can be your companion or your enemy*
*The mind...Your mind*
*Have you used it, or is it in a state of limbo?*
*Do you take care not to damage and destroy it?*
*The mind...your mind...is a powerful tool*
*If you use it*
*Ira Carol, 4-6-04*

"An idle mind is the devil's workshop," is an old saying that is still being used today. If you allow an automobile to idle in a garage, the garage becomes inhabitable. We did not allow our children's minds to be idle. As I wrote earlier, a child's mind is like a sponge. It soaks up everything it comes into contact with, good or bad, positive or negative.

I attended a wedding fifteen years ago and was annoyed by a four or five-year-old child who was allowed to do whatever he wanted, including turning over glasses filled with beverages. The young parents just watched and did nothing to attempt to control this child. The father ultimately made the comment, "Just wait until you get older, I'm really going to whip your butt." When the child gets older, it's too late. Unfortunately, he'll probably be whipping his dad's butt.

*Ira Carol and Anthony shortly after his birth in 1979.*

On February 6, 2001, I was in a restaurant waiting to pick up a carryout food order. A woman came out of the restroom with a child, who looked to be about four-years-old. I do not know what the child had done, but this woman said to her, "If you do that again, I'll break your arm." Disciplining a child begins before he starts to walk and continues until he becomes a young adult. There are many ways to teach and discipline your children. Do not ignore them, or threaten to break their arms. Intimidation does nothing but teach them that violence is an acceptable method of control. If parents on a consistent basis use this control mechanism, children will learn to use violence as a means of controlling people.

# A Father's Triumphant Story

In 2010, 13,186 people died in terrorist attacks worldwide; in the same year, in America alone, 31,672 people lost their lives in gun-related deaths, according to numbers compiled by Tom Diaz—until recently, a senior analyst at the Violence Policy Center. *(Samuel Burke, CNN, January 15, 2013)*

How much of this violence can be attributed to parents, or the absence of parents? I am not sure if this can be measured, but I do know that households where parents are intricately involved in every aspect of their child's life can help to prevent such violence.

The child-raising window of opportunity is narrow. No one can predict how positive or negative a child will become, but as parents, you must strive to raise your children to be the best that they can be. You must do everything within your power to raise your child. This is a difficult and time consuming task, but you must give it your best effort. It is a life or death challenge, which parents must meet head on. If you place your child in positive environments, the odds are he will become a positive person. Place him in negative environments; the odds are he will become a negative person. Do nothing and the child will do whatever he wants and will not be able to differentiate between good and evil, positive or negative.

The guidance provided by parents, relatives, friends, or guardians, is crucial for the positive development of any child. Parents must be willing to spend the time, energy, and money to raise their children. It's a huge responsibility, which must not be taken lightly. Raising children is a full time job. Don't take this job for granted and please don't be part time parents.

Reading was a major activity in our home. Before they could walk or talk, Demarre and Anthony had their own collection of cloth books. Demarre was eight-months-old when he took his first steps. Anthony started walking at ten months. They were both walking around carrying and chewing on their books before

204

they started talking. Before they started school, both sons loved to read and spent hours reading silently in their bedrooms. It seemed that every week we were either in a library or a bookstore, searching for that exciting never-ending adventure story. We read to Demarre and Anthony every day. They came to expect the reading sessions. "Read me a bedtime story," became a normal request of them, although this was not the only time of day we read to our sons. On many nights, I would be reading to one son and Ira Carol would be reading to the other. Many times we all were sprawled out on our bed reading to each other. Read to small children and you will ultimately see a role reversal. They will soon be reading to you.

> Today I stayed over my grandmother's house. My cousin's baby brother came to stay. I was playing with him. I rode him around in the stroller. I watched TV, and read books. Anthony McGill, 12-22-87

The child who is allowed to write his own daily schedule, or "do his own thing," will ultimately allow other people outside of the home to dictate what activities he gets involved in. Parents must be aware of who their child's friends are, and where he is when not at home. This is not saying that we must place a tracking device on him, but it is of vital importance that parents know where the child is, and who he is with. You will not always know this, but you must make every attempt to know, especially during his preteen and teen years. Establish ground rules early in his life. Make him understand that you are concerned about his well-being. Most importantly, let him know that love is the reason for your madness.

There is no magic formula for raising successful children. But there are many principles or tools a parent can use. Find and use them from birth until they become independent adults.

*Christmas at Uncle Jim's and Aunt Jelly's house.*

# CHAPTER FIFTEEN

## TV AND THE NEGATIVE
## NINTENDO INFLUENCE

To create a balance in their lives, Ira Carol and I attempted to provide our sons with educational and fun activities. We kept them active without overworking them. These activities also served to keep them off the streets of Chicago and away from the gangs that controlled certain sections of the city.

Although they had many positive friends who they socialized with, Demarre and Anthony didn't have time to hang out with the boys on the corner or playground. They didn't have time to spend hours playing video games, although my wife and I were captivated by the Nintendo craze when this product hit the market.

Because of overwhelming consumer interest, game consoles were selling out as soon as they arrived in the stores. In our attempt to purchase this game as a Christmas gift for our sons, we drove hundreds of miles to various stores throughout Indiana and Illinois. We finally found and bought one for about one hundred twenty-four dollars.

Shortly after purchasing the game system and several games, Ira Carol and I laid out some basic ground rules related to when they could be played, and for what length of time. We also instructed our sons to not take the games to school. Demarre and Anthony agreed to these rules and regulations.

I tried playing the games with my sons, but my thumbs always got in the way. My attempt to learn to play failed, and I stopped trying. Unfortunately, Demarre didn't stop. He became obsessed with playing Mario Brothers and some of the other non-violent Nintendo games. He was not the only teenager, who was hooked on Nintendo. My wife discovered there was an almost cult like underground Nintendo game swapping and selling business going on at Kenwood Academy.

One day after Ira Carol and I returned home from work, Demarre told us he lost one of the games somewhere in our house. We did not think much of this loss and figured the game would probably be found. A month or so later, Anthony approached his mother and said, "Mama, Lavelle found the Nintendo game behind the clothes dryer in the basement." We thought this was strange because he was playing with the newly found game, although our basement had recently flooded as a result of a major rainstorm.

About one week later, Demarre asked us for permission to attend a school function. Ira Carol called Demarre's locker partner's mother to find out if her son was also going. Mrs. Smith immediately said, "I am so glad you called. Did Demarre get the money my son left him for the lost Nintendo game?" Ira Carol had no idea what Mrs. Smith was talking about. She soon discovered that Demarre had taken games to school to loan or trade with other students. His locker partner lost one of his game. After some intense questioning of Demarre, we discovered that he had gone to another student at school and bought the same game he previously said he lost.

Ira Carol, the family investigator, went to the seller's home and spoke to his mother. She discovered that the student who was selling Nintendo games did not own a Nintendo game console. He was selling his neighbor's and friend's games. Ira Carol discovered that Nintendo was big business at Kenwood Academy, where students were trading and selling these games all over the school.

After completing the investigation, my wife and I had a serious talk with our sons. We discussed the serious consequences of lying, and the importance of telling the truth. As a result of this incident, Demarre had to write a two-page essay on how this situation happened and how he could have avoided it. The following is the first page of his essay:

## The Event That Changed My Life

I tell ya, when things go wrong they really go wrong. Trying to cover up for a friend gets me in trouble. Let me explain:

It all started when I let Khaalis borrow my *Legend of Zelda*. He kept it for about 1 week when suddenly he came to me and said he lost it. I told him he would have to pay me the money. I didn't tell my mother and father what happened, in fear that Khaalis would be in trouble. I feel that if Khaalis would have told me that he told his mother, I would have told mine because his mother understood. Instead I ended up being the person that would get in trouble. It was about a week and a half when Khaalis paid me the money. During lunch of that same day, I found the money missing. Soon summer came and I still didn't have the money nor the Zelda. It was not until the beginning of the school year I really started saving for it. I already had about $2.00. I figured if I saved for about 1½ months I would have enough and my life would…

I am still looking for the second page of this essay. It would be fun to see how he ended this story. Again, we used this incident as a teachable moment. This Nintendo fever had a temporary negative effect on Demarre's music making. He stopped practicing his flute. His life seemed to center around the game. Ira Carol and I decided to sell it. We found a parent who purchased the Nintendo console for the same price we paid for it.

Demarre was extremely upset, but soon began to practice his flute again. To this day, I believe the decision to sell the Nintendo console and games was a major turning point in his life, and caused him to refocus his mind toward music.

*As I was driving Anthony to school several months after we sold the Nintendo, he turned towards me and asked,* 'Mama, why did you sell the game? I liked playing it too and you didn't think of me.' *I explained to Anthony that he was a victim of circumstances. I knew he was not the one who broke the rules, but he lived in the house where the rules were broken, and unfortunately, that Nintendo game had to be sold. Anthony didn't like it, but I felt that he would eventually adjust to the outcome. I also explained to Anthony that if he went to a store with a friend and that friend got caught stealing, most likely, he would be arrested with his friend. I tried to explain the concept 'guilt by association.' Anthony finished this conversation by saying* 'I understand.'

*Be aware of your child's outside, and inside the home activities. To create a balance between school, play, and family outings, you may have to change your child's activities. Ira Carol*

In order for parents and children to have time to talk to each other, priorities have to be established. The almighty television should be on the lowest rung of any family's priority list. Many parents allow their children's lives to center around the television, which gives them unrealistic views of the world they live in. I don't mean to insinuate that all television is negative, but it is a known fact that there is too much sex and violence being programmed for television. Parents should not allow their children to watch this stuff.

On October 28, 2003, the Kaiser Family Foundation and Children's Digital Media Centers, released findings of a study relative to children and television watching. This study found that children who live in homes where watching television is a primary activity, or where televisions are on during long periods of the day, develop reading problems and have difficulty learning to read. There have been many other studies that have reached the same conclusions.

By the time they reach adulthood, some children have watched thousands of murders and sex acts on television. Controls must be placed on this so-called entertainment device. Limits should be placed on any child's television viewing. Make television watching a family affair. Take the television out of the child's bedroom and place it in the family room, or a common area of the home. Instead of throwing the TV guide out with the other recyclables, use it as a scheduling tool and as reading material for your child. Use the cable television broadcast guide now being shown directly on the television screen to look for positive programs to watch. There are many excellent programs on television. The Discovery Channel, the History Channel, National Geographic Channel, and programs on the Public Broadcasting Service are four of them. There are many more positive shows available, but parents must search for them. The time spent ensuring that your child is watching positive and educational programs is priceless.

It is a known fact that the amount of sex and violence shown on television, in movies, video games, and in society as a whole, has increased considerably. It is not uncommon for hundreds of murders to be shown on television in such gruesome bloody detail that it makes some adults cover their eyes.

The number of actual murders that take place in schools has also increased substantially over the past several years. The April 20, 1999 violent acts of two teenagers in Colorado, killed fourteen high school students and one teacher. The students who committed these crimes were considered to be loners who spent many hours playing one of the most violent video games on the market. The fact that these young men had access to guns led to this tragedy. These students were followers of several rock music groups who use extreme violence in their lyrics and stage performances. They made bombs in their bedrooms, and filmed themselves shooting shotguns and semi-automatic weapons in a wooded area near their homes. The guns were kept in the teenager's bedrooms.

Another gruesome video game related murder occurred in October of 2007, when an Ohio sixteen-year-old teenager killed his mother and wounded his father because they took his video game away from him. This teenager was found guilty of aggravated murder and attempted aggravated murder. According to a news article distributed by the Associated Press, he also loved to play one of the most violent video games on the market. In my opinion, these games are deadly. Don't purchase them for your children. Don't allow them to play these games, or associate with other children who do.

On December 14, 2012, a twenty-year-old man armed with two semi-automatic handguns and an assault rifle, forced his way into Sandy Hook Elementary School, located in Newtown, Connecticut. The gunman murdered twenty children aged six and seven, and six adult staff members. This incident has caused many in this country to question the easy availability of assault weapons. Because of the power of many of the gun lobbying groups, it's questionable if our politicians have the will to fix this problem.

In 2013, gun violence among adults and teenagers continues to take an extraordinary toll on young and old. This violence has reached epidemic proportions. As a direct result of gun violence, over 30,000 people in the United States die each year. In my own city of Chicago, gun violence is destroying the lives of too many children and adults. It is time for America to stand up and admit that this is a serious problem, which needs to be addressed–now.

Another problem that is escalating at an alarming rate is teenage suicides. As parents, we must talk to our children to ensure that their precious lives are not being shattered by outside forces, or internal confusion.

On March 4, 2008, while driving home from the local grocery store, a radio station was playing a speech by presidential candidate Senator Barack Obama talking about gun violence in United States. The following is a quote from Mr. Obama: "From South Central, L.A., to Newark, New Jersey, there's an epidemic of violence that's sickening the soul of this nation," the Illinois senator told the crowd. "The violence is unacceptable and it's got to stop." Nearly three dozen students were killed by violence during the 2007 school year, according to Chicago Public School officials. Senator Obama said that figure is higher than the number of Illinois servicemen who died in Iraq in 2007. "We need to express our collective anger through collective action," Senator Obama said.

As parents or guardians of children, you must monitor the people they associate with. You must, to the greatest extent possible, monitor all aspects of your children's lives; who their friends are, where they are going when they enter the universe of the World Wide Web, the games they play on computers, and the music they listen to. This sounds like an impossible task, but it is one that parents must diligently undertake.

Without being shadows of your children, be aware of their whereabouts when they are outside of the home, or searching the Internet. All of the above are keys related to RAISING positive and

*Demarre McGill photo by Darin Fong.*

successful children. Parents must be realistic and understand that everything involved in raising children will not be a positive experience. Use the positives and negatives as teaching opportunities. Don't become so negative that you miss the chance to teach because of your overreaction. Communicate with the parents of your child's friends. Insist on communicating with them in person, via telephone, and by email. This creates an extended family, and helps to protect everyone involved, especially the children.

Parents must recognize negative activities and behavioral changes in their children, investigate and find the possible causes, and take immediate action when necessary. These actions are also keys to raising your children. Use them to unlock the positive energies and creativity found within all children. Don't be surprised when they start to excel in the classroom, and during extracurricular activities. Take pride in knowing that you were there when they needed you the most.

*President-elect Barack Obama before being sworn in.*
*January 20, 2009 photo by D. McGill.*

# CHAPTER SIXTEEN

## THE MOST AMAZING PHONE
## CALL OF MY LIFE

On December 17, 2008, I was sitting in my big Chevy conver-
sion van in the parking lot of the local grocery store when I
received a telephone call from Anthony. The first words out of his
mouth were, "Hi Daddy. Are you sitting down?" Before answering
him, I immediately started wondering what the good news was, for
our sons always share news of their accomplishments with us. I told
Anthony that I was sitting. He slowly and deliberately informed me

that the manager of the great cellist, Yo-Yo Ma, called and asked if he was available to perform with him. I screamed and said, "Man, what an honor."

Anthony informed me that he was scheduled to perform in Amsterdam and would have to call there to get released from this job. He was able to reach the people in Amsterdam and they told him that he could book the Ma engagement. He called Ma's manager and informed him that he could do the performance. Anthony was then told that he would be performing live at the inauguration of President-elect Barack Obama. When he told me that he was playing a new piece by John Williams with Yo-Yo Ma, Itzak Perlman, and Gabriela Montero, I screamed, "You have got to be kidding me." He also told me not to mention this to anyone.

Anthony was just as excited as I was. I told him that this did not surprise me because I knew how hard he had worked to be considered one of the finest clarinetists in the business. Anthony has been playing the clarinet for more than twenty-five years and worked diligently to become a world-class musician. I told him that he should expect more calls like this because he has prepared himself for any musical challenge.

I called Ira Carol to give her the good news and of course Anthony had already spoken to her-mothers first. She was elated and we ended up screaming at each other over the phone one more time. We eventually started talking normally. We talked about our sons and our lives for about thirty-five minutes and finally said goodbye. I have never been one to talk on the telephone for over five minutes, unless it was a business call when I was working, but this long conversation with my wife did not bother me at all.

The next day, December 18, 2008, Anthony called me again. He said, "It's official." I asked him, "What's official?" He immediately said, "The news about the inauguration is in the New

York Times." He also mentioned that the Joint Congressional Committee on Inaugural Ceremonies had released the inaugural program to the world and his name was on it. I nervously turned on my notebook computer and started searching. I found the official website. My heart started pounding (again) when I saw my son's name immediately above President-elect Obama's name on the program. I thought, could this be real? I eventually calmed down by telling myself, yes, it is real, and it is not surprising. I then pulled out my cell phone and did what any proud parent would have done, started calling every person in my contact list.

Anthony and his brother Demarre travelled to Chicago the following week and we all spent some quality time together during the Christmas holiday. What a thrill it was to talk about old times and to look at some of the many old photographs in our collection. To hear Anthony talk about his upcoming gig with Yo-Yo Ma, Perlman, and Montero was awesome. He later said to us, "I might be able to get inauguration tickets for close family members." We had no idea that at the inauguration, we would be sitting approximately one hundred feet from the President of the United States of America. After returning home to Manhattan, Anthony called to inform me that the Joint Committee offered him four tickets to the inauguration. I am going to the inauguration, wow, what a thought! Demarre, my nephew Marcus, and Abby would also be attending. I bought my plane ticket from Southwest Airlines and placed the printed confirmation information on the dresser in my bedroom.

Anthony called about two weeks before the inauguration to inform me that he received an email from the Joint Committee informing him that he could purchase up to five tickets to the Obama Home States Inaugural Ball. He jumped on this opportunity immediately.

Now I had to shop for a new tuxedo because my old one had shrunk to a ridiculously small size. This is the excuse I use anyway.

It took me a couple of days of sloshing around in partially melted snow on the South and North sides of Chicago, but I eventually found the perfect tux and accessories. When I got that new tux home and tried in on, I felt proud to be the father of two great young African American men and the husband of a beautiful woman and great mother.

My flight was scheduled to depart Midway Airport at 1:40 P.M. on January 19, 2009. The night before my departure, I realized that I had not ordered tickets for Marcus and me to get from BWI to Union Station in Washington D. C. I quickly retrieved my computer and searched for Amtrak. I opened the Amtrak reservations page and submitted the appropriate information. As I scrolled down the different departure times, I was shocked to discover they were all sold out! I almost panicked. I grabbed my cell phone and called Marcus and asked him to start searching Amtrak's site for seats. I also suggested that he ask James to search on yet another computer. My heart was pounding, and I was starting to visualize us being stranded at the BWI Amtrak station during the inauguration.

Forecasters were saying that over two million people would be in Washington on the twentieth, and I thought one million of them would be trying to get into Washington at the same time as me and Marcus. I am now in full panic mode. James increased my anxiety by refusing to get involved in this ticket search game. I called him a few choice names and continued to search the site. To my surprise, I found a link stating that two seats were available on the 6:25 P.M. train to Union Station and I purchased them as fast as I could. The fifty dollars per seat did not faze me. I just wanted to get to D. C., "by any means necessary." *(Malcolm X, June 1964)*

My friend Steve picked me up at 10:30 A.M. on January 19. He was driving his mother's silver Dodge Caravan. He insisted on picking me up so early to avoid the massive crowd we expected at the airport. On our way to the airport, it seemed like Steve was driving only five miles per hour. I was about to tell him to drive faster, but my subconscious mind told me to relax. We arrived at Midway at 11:05 A.M. and said our goodbyes with the traditional fist bump. Steve sped off and I extended the handle on my luggage bag and continued to the bag check section of Southwest Airlines. To my amazement, the airport was not crowded, although I did have to stand in line for about fifteen minutes before reaching the kiosk and ticket agent. After checking in, the agent handed me my luggage check ticket folder after she scribbled the number B-26 on it. I looked at my phone to get the time and realized I was two hours ahead of my scheduled departure.

Before going to gate B-26, I stopped at a bar and grill, pulled a tall end stool out and placed my carry-on bag on the floor next to it. My super sharp new navy blue Dobbs hat with the turned down brim was placed on top of the bag. I bought this hat a week earlier. It reminded me of the good old days during the seventies and eighties when I thought I was the best-dressed dude on the South Side of Chicago.

My mind kept thinking about the enormous historical event I was about to witness. The thoughts racing through my mind were overwhelming. The bartender passed me a menu that caused me to switch from thoughts of the inauguration and Anthony's role, to food. The veggie burger was good, but the golden brown wedge potatoes were even better. I washed the food down with a glass of cabernet and a cup of ice water with a slice of lemon.

One hour and fifteen minutes before departure, my heart was beating too fast, but I did all I could to maintain my exterior calm demeanor. I wondered if the people sitting to my left could hear my heart beating. I surely could. The time went by very fast and the agent started to call A group to board.

After about half an hour, all passengers were finally in their seats. I pushed my earplugs into my ears to prevent the ear pain I usually experience during flights and especially during landings.

The earplugs also provided some solitude from the muffled noises on the plane. This attempt to just relax didn't work. The woman sitting next to me started talking about the inauguration and could not stop. I pulled the earplug from my left ear and carried on a conversation with this stranger for about twenty minutes. My relief came when the woman sitting in the aisle seat entered the conversation. What a relief that was. I put the earplug back into my ear, closed my eyes and dozed off. I hope I didn't snore too loudly. I awoke as the pilot was announcing that we were approaching BWI.

My nephew Marcus met me at baggage check. He drove from Timonium, Maryland and parked his car in the extended stay lot. We hugged and followed the signs to the area where a red and white bus picked up passengers and shuttled them to the Amtrak/MARC train station. Before Marcus and I boarded the Amtrak/MARC bus, I talked to an information officer whose workstation was located just inside the doors where the buses were parked. I told this man that we were trying to get to the Amtrak station. He asked if we had tickets. I informed him that I purchased Amtrak tickets for fifty dollars each the night before. He said that we could have purchased tickets for the MARC train for six dollars. This train uses the same tracks as Amtrak, but makes a few more stops. Too late. I didn't care. We got seats to D. C.

The train was packed with people, all seemingly caught up in inauguration euphoria. After about thirty or thirty-five minutes, the train pulled into Union Station. As we departed the train, I couldn't help but notice an end car on another track that had the traditional red, white, and blue bunting draped over a railing. Was this the train that President-elect Obama took to Delaware to pick up Vice President-elect Biden? This thought stayed with me for a few minutes after which Marcus and I became part of an endless mass of people pulling luggage bags and attempting to find an exit from the Capitol side of Union Station. After talking to three different police officers, we finally made it out of the station mad house.

The congestion was worse on the street. People were everywhere. Marcus and I maneuvered our way out of the mass of humanity and pulled out our maps. The huge Capitol Building was glowing in front of us and we used it as a landmark to get our bearings.

It was impossible to get a cab or catch public transportation so we decided to start walking. With the help of more police officers, we made all the right turns and after walking for about forty minutes, we arrived at the Capitol Hill Suites Hotel. My feet were killing me and I don't know if I could have walked another block.

This was a very cold night. It felt like we had walked five miles instead of a few city blocks. My biggest concern during the walk to the hotel was not the cold or my tired feet. I was thinking about Marcus's health. James donated one of his kidneys to his son, who at the time, was on the verge of total renal failure. Marcus was living in Atlanta with his mother. Three times every week he had to undergo dialysis treatment. James saved his son's life by giving him a kidney. During the walk, I constantly asked Marcus if he was healthy enough to continue. Each time he looked at me, smiled and said, "I'm fine Uncle D." This is another example of a parent doing whatever was necessary to provide for his child, no matter what age.

As we opened the door to the hotel and entered, there seemed to be about fifteen to twenty people jammed into the small lobby. They all said hello to us at the same time. We acknowledged their greetings and proceeded straight toward the elevators, and upon entering; I punched the number five button. After exiting the elevator and turning a couple of corners, we finally arrived at room 521.

Anthony and Abby greeted us with smiling faces and big hugs. We made it, cold feet and all. Demarre arrived at about 1:30 A.M. from San Diego, California.

At about 7:30 the morning of the inauguration, Anthony opened the door of his bedroom and hollered out, "We need to get ready." We lay motionless for a few more minutes and finally started to move around on the sofa bed and the floor. After rationing the remaining clean towels, we took our turn in the small bathroom. The bundle up phase of the trip started to kick in.

At 9:00 A.M., Anthony received a phone call from the front desk that our transportation to the inauguration ceremony was waiting for us. Anthony, Abby, Marcus, Demarre, and I quickly finished dressing. After looking in the mirror, we all dashed to the lobby where we were met by our escort and two D. C. police officers who wiped us down with a digital security wand–between the legs, down the arms, around the shoulders and back. The lobby was again full of people, all seemed to be staring at us. I guess they were wondering who the heck we were. We all passed this exam and were escorted to a long white passenger van containing the families of Yo-Yo Ma and Gabriela Montero. In front of and behind our van were two police cars with emergency lights activated. After we were all seated, the sirens of the police cars were turned on and we raced off toward the Capitol Building. Both sides of the street were packed with people and it seemed as though everyone was staring at our little motorcade. My eyes became watery as I gazed at the thousands of people.

It took only about a minute to arrive on the North side of the Capitol Building. This was perhaps the most exiting ride of my life. Although my camera was secure in my hands with the strap draped around my neck, I forgot to take pictures. I guess I was caught up in the excitement of this inauguration experience that I was a part of.

After exiting the van and going through another four security checkpoints, we finally arrived at the bleachers erected on the steps of the Capitol. Anthony was escorted into the Capitol Building and the four of us mortals continued to the upper level of the bleachers.

The temperature was twenty-three degrees Fahrenheit when we arrived and the extra chemical hand warmers we got from the escort really helped, but our feet didn't fare as well. At 9:45 A.M., we had been on the scene for only half an hour, but everyone agreed that the thirty minutes seemed more like two hours. Upon arrival at the bleachers, we actually sat down, but soon realized that our bodies felt warmer when we were standing. This was probably caused by the more efficient blood flow and the fact that we were constantly moving while standing. Soon, all the people around us were standing and moving their bodies. Everybody was complaining about the cold weather, while at the same time, smiling about the historical event that was about to take place.

Ira Carol was not with us at President Obama's inauguration. Ironically, she was in Louisville, Kentucky performing in *Brothers of a Common Country,* a professional theatre production.

*Photo of Ira Carol and cast performing in Deborah Lyn Frockt's,* Brothers of a Common Country, *a play about President Abraham Lincoln and Frederick Douglass. Courtesy of StageOne Family Theatre, Louisville, Kentucky.*

The play was a story about the lives of President Abraham Lincoln and the great abolitionist Frederick Douglass, written by Deborah Lyn Frockt to celebrate President Lincoln's 200th birthday.

Abraham Lincoln, Frederick Douglass, and Dr. Martin Luther King, Jr., were all with us spiritually on this history-making day. Ira Carol was indeed with us; she was watching the inauguration on a television set in her backstage dressing room.

This was truly an amazing time for all of us. How interesting it was that on the day Illinois Senator Barack Obama became the 44th President of the United States of America, Ira Carol was performing in a theatrical production about President Abraham Lincoln, the President who issued the Emancipation Proclamation on January 1, 1863. This Proclamation freed the slaves and made it possible for Barack Obama to become President of the United States of America.

*Anthony McGill*

It is still amazing that our son Anthony performed at President Barack Obama's first inauguration. I wonder if President Lincoln or Frederick Douglass ever thought about the possibility of a black man with a Kenyan father, and a white American mother becoming President of the United States. Dr. King surely did.

Our vantage point for this historic occasion was the highest of any of the spectators or seated guest, except the ones on the roofs of some of the far away high-rise buildings. The view was incredible. When I looked out at the mass of people that stretched from the Capitol steps all the way beyond the Washington Monument, another chill went down my spine. I felt like I was truly on Dr. Martin Luther King's mountaintop. This is what Dr. King envisioned in 1963, and talked about again in a 1968 speech one day before he died.

The various colored dots representing the individual people stretched out in front of us reminded me of a Jackson Pollack painting. Beyond the people sitting in folding chairs on the lawn of the Capitol, I could not see faces, only colors. Red, white, black, and blue dots were predominant throughout the mass of people. I could not believe that the National Mall was already filled with two million people. I will never forget this sight. I made sure of this by taking five hundred photos with my Sony A-100 camera. A couple of days before I arrived in Washington, Anthony was informed by the Joint Committee that he and a guest were invited to be in the President's reviewing stand during the parade. Anthony was told that he would actually be inside the heated enclosure of the reviewing stand with the President. I would have to view the parade from an open area next to the reviewing stand, but Anthony and I could change places periodically. The Joint Committee received my credentials from Anthony–social security number, birthplace, and other information. This was necessary so the Secret Service could perform security background checks.

When the inaugural ceremony concluded with the benediction by Reverend Joseph Lowery, Demarre, Marcus, Abby, and I met our escort outside of the Capitol security zone. I had forgotten where the staging area was located. We called Anthony and had to go through the security checkpoints again. By this time we were still freezing and our feet were throbbing. Demarre had a weird walk going on. I was behind him and he looked like he had just gotten off a horse he had been riding for hours. Obviously his feet were freezing and hurting. His were not the only hurting feet in our group.

We met our escort and were led to a small room inside the Capitol Building. As soon as we walked into this room, Yo-Yo Ma greeted and hugged each of us. Anthony and Montero and a few other people were also in the room. Yo-Yo brought me a cup of hot coffee and it seems we all were talking about the cold weather and how nice it was to be in a warm room.

We warmed up for about ten minutes and were escorted out because the buses back to the hotel and to the inaugural parade were starting to load. On the way out, I marveled at the beautiful interior of the Capitol. The detailed mosaic artwork imbedded into the archways and walls was astonishing.

We passed Reverend Lowery who was talking to a man while sitting in his wheel chair. I thought about photographing him, but out of respect, I didn't bother. I didn't think about getting Yo-Yo Ma's and Gabriela Montero's autographs until I returned to the hotel. I guess I was too frozen and engrossed in the moment to think about an autograph. Anthony and I were escorted out of the building and walked about a block to the buses, staged and ready to transport people to the parade. Demarre, Abby, and Marcus were escorted to the long white passenger van that transported them back to the Capitol Hills Suites. Anthony and I found our bus with the yellow sticker affixed to the inside of the passenger side windshield. The bus was almost full. We strutted back toward the rear where we found two empty seats. We looked at each other and were glad to be on a warm bus.

We joked about the fact that it seemed that the special treatment we had been receiving was over. There was nothing personal about being on a bus with fifty other passengers. We asked each other if we really wanted to spend another three or four hours at the parade after three and a half hours at the inauguration. This question was answered when Anthony realized that the two parade tickets were inside his clarinet case, which he had given to Abby. This oversight answered all of our questions. We again looked at each other and immediately got up and started walking toward the front exit door.

Some of the other passengers shouted, "Are you all leaving?" Anthony responded, "We forgot our tickets," and kept walking. We walked from the bus back to the hotel. At the time, Anthony and I were glad that he had forgotten the tickets. This gave us the oppor- tunity to warm up and to rest before the Obama Home States Ball. I still wonder if Anthony and I would have met President Barack Obama if we had stayed on that bus. One thing is certain, we will never know.

By 7:45 P.M., we all were starting to get dressed for the Obama Home States Ball. My niece LaShelle arrived and seemed to be excited about attending the ball. LaShelle and her children Demitrios and T'Ahna arrived in our room at 4:00 A.M. to drop off her clothes and to use the bathroom. They then left to take their spot on the Mall with the two million other people. There were so many people on the Mall at 5:00 A.M., LaShelle and family had to wind their way down to the Washington Monument before finding a space with breathing room. Because Anthony was only able to secure five ball tickets, Marcus decided to remain in the room so that LaShelle could attend.

Anthony came out of the bedroom with his black and white bow tie already tied. He approached his brother, handed him an all black bow tie and began to demonstrate to him how to tie it. Demarre learned the technique quickly and in a few minutes he was smiling in front of the large bathroom mirror. The bow tying demo seemed easy to follow, but I was in no mood to learn how by untying Demarre's. I liked the look of a *real* bow tie and promised myself to purchase some when I arrived back in Chicago. The promise was broken, for I have yet to buy one of these ties.

After dressing, we all stood around the hotel room for a few minutes of picture taking. We were tired but our smiles were still in place. We all piled out of the room and boarded the nearest elevator for the trip to the lobby. As soon as we exited the elevator, several people noticed Anthony and immediately shouted "Great music" and "Good job." The weather was cold this night. None of us was dressed for the low temperature that seemed to be in the teens. The long blue and white bus we boarded was packed with people, but we all were able to find seats, although none of us was able to sit together. Listening to the chatter on the bus revealed that several of the people were politicians. They seemed to want us to know this.

We finally arrived at the convention center and had to again brave the cold. The bus did not drop us off at the entrance; instead, the driver parked almost a block away. Because we were late, all of us started running toward the entrance. We didn't want to miss seeing the President and the First Lady dance. It seemed like we ran a mile through the streets and the convention center, but we did get a chance to see the President and his beautiful wife. We caught the end of their slow romantic dance. After the music ended, the large crowd erupted into a loud emotional cheer. The President and First Lady stood center stage smiling and waving to the people.

A short time after President Obama and his wife left the stage, Vice President Joe Biden and wife, Dr. Jill Biden, walked out waving and smiling. They also did a slow dance. This couple really seemed to be enjoying themselves. They remained on stage for several minutes and seemed happy to be celebrating with the people who put them in this glorious position.

Standing there in this room full of people and watching the President and Vice President was one of the most exciting times of my life. The feeling was completely surreal. I thought about the great African Americans who made tremendous sacrifices to make this day possible. I felt as though all of them; Sojourner Truth, W. E. B. DuBois, Frederick Douglass, Whitney Young, George Washington Carver, Harriet Tubman, Booker T. Washington, Roy Wilkins, Malcolm X, Thurgood Marshall, Ida B. Wells, Vernon Jarrett, Dr. Martin Luther King Jr., and all the *contributors to the cause,* were here. On January 20, 2009, the spirits of all these heroes were on Dr. King's mountaintop, relishing the historical event that had just taken place.

Parents should remember, when it comes to raising children, anything is possible if you do all that you can to take control of the process yourself. Be there with your children every step of the journey and take the time every day to teach. Let your children know that they can be whatever they want to be if they work hard, even the President of the United States of America.

In a December 2011 article published in *The New York Flute Club's* newsletter, Demarre was asked: "...if being an African American had factored into his experience as a classical musician?" He responded as follows:

> Of course it has. But I believe that everyone's culture, family life, and past experiences make their perspective a unique one. When I am making music, I am not thinking of whether the music is black or white. I am simply trying to make great music. I am aware that my race becomes a very important factor when I am doing outreach in black and Latino communities. It is critical that young black and Latino children are made aware that they can do anything they set their minds to,

including becoming a classical musician. *(New York Flute Club, December 2011)*

## *A STITCH IN TIME*

*Our lives are like stitches in time. Throughout our lives we are constantly stitching our own patterns during a relative short lifetime. Our lives are undeniably a part of a whole interwoven pattern of different stitches, some our own and some belonging to others. We go through life not truly understanding how these stitches and patterns fit or where our stitch is. Some of us use so much energy trying to find out what lies ahead and end up missing or not realizing their stitch has ended.*

*I know that life is your plan and we all tend to jump the gun and not ask or seek your guidance along the way. Before we realize it, we're at the finish line. God, I've seen so much yet so little when I really think about the scope of things as they are related to the universe. Friends and family members have passed by us, each completing his stitch as it is linked to someone else. Some patterns were much shorter and others were longer, but they all crossed at some point and added to the overall pattern of this thing we call life. This huge pattern is the universal framework of life.*

*In this life, God sews our stitches. He tugs at our needle, and at other needles along the way. He gently touches these needles and the stitch moves slowly along the pattern. Each individual is a part of this universal pattern, and each is more interwoven throughout it than we might think.*

*We are so grateful to be a part of other people's patterns, whether they are friend or foe. We are eternally grateful to have had other stitches in time cross our paths and patterns.*

*Parents, to ensure the successful and positive development of your children, the stitches that are a part of your life patterns should be interwoven with those of your children. To complete the pattern and help children start and continue their stitches, your guidance, love, and support must be there to lead them, every stitch of the way. Ira Carol*

Don't neglect your children, you have them for a short period of time and then they are gone. Use this time to love, to teach, to nourish, and to raise your children. This will be one of the most difficult jobs of your life, but could be one of the most rewarding periods of time you will experience in your lifetime. Cherish the few years as you raise your sons to be men and your daughters to be women. They will use the knowledge taught by you to raise their own children.

Ira Carol and I are not grandparents yet, but we are sure our sons will raise beautiful, successful children (if they ever desire to have children), using some of the same techniques and key principles we used to raise them.

On January 28, 2009, Classical music writer and author Norman Lebrecht wrote the following in his weekly column called *Lebrecht Weekly:*

> At his inauguration, four classical musicians were given a few freezing moments to show...that the new president has got more than rock, jazz and rap on his (music player). Anthony McGill, 29, who played the clarinet...is a classic example of empowerment through art-a fireman's son who rose through Chicago schools to hold a principal's seat in the Met Orchestra.
>
> His brother, Demarre, equally determined, is principal flute in San Diego. Men like the McGills are the music behind Obama's message of hope. *(Norman Lebrecht)*

Yes, candidate Obama made hope a major part of his campaign rhetoric. During the campaign he stated, "Anything is possible in America." Candidate Obama was correct. He is now the President of the United States of America. Ira Carol and I constantly told our sons the same thing. Throughout a child's life, parents should constantly tell their children that anything is possible and that all their goals are reachable if they believe in themselves and work hard toward achieving those goals.

*Anthony, Abby Fennessy, LaShelle Woodson, and Demarre*
*at President Obama's 2009 Home States Ball.*

On February 1, 2011, Anthony wrote the following:

This past weekend I had the honor to play the Brahms Clarinet Trio with Yo-Yo Ma and Emanuel Ax at Symphony Center in Chicago. It was a wonderful experience. The concert was the pinnacle of a weekend celebrating the launch of the Yo-Yo Ma/Chicago Symphony's Citizen Musician Initiative.

The concept is a wonderfully simple one to grasp and hopefully will begin a movement to spread the gift of music to the largest amount of people. We went around to different places in the city, played, talked and spread music and friendship all over the place.

So what did I do exactly and why is it important?

I woke up Saturday (1-29-11) and went to the Parkway Community Center and played for and talked with kids about the power of music and what meaning it had in my life. I had fun just spending time together and letting them know that I discovered at their age what I loved to do and went for it all the way.

I grew up on the South Side of Chicago and I understand the struggles of so many young people. We discussed how you can focus your energies on positive people and positive endeavors to achieve your goals in life. My medium was music, but the process is the same in all areas of life. *(Anthony McGill's Blog 2-1-11)*

Parents, it doesn't matter who you are, where you live, or how much money you have. With your unwavering love, dedication, and support, your children can be whomever and whatever they desire: a great musician, doctor, teacher, astronaut, nurse, carpenter, and even the President of the United States of America.

On December 17, 2011, I saw firsthand a real life visualization that many African American fathers and mothers are raising their children, and just as Ira Carol and I did, they are attending their performances. Our neighbors gave us tickets to attend their daughter's elementary school's holiday program at Harlan Community Academy located on the South Side of Chicago. The two-hour program was inspiring. It seemed as if the entire student body of McDade Elementary Classical School participated in the program. At times there were thirty or forty students—from the smallest to the largest—on stage. The singing and acting was extraordinary for such young students.

What impressed me most was the number of African American adult males and young children in the audience. This was definitely a family affair. About 2,000 people packed the auditorium. African American men seemed to fill more than half the seats. Many men with small children in tow walked the aisles looking for a place to sit. At one point, I stood up and scanned the audience with my wide-open eyes. The view from the rear was beautiful. I think this is happening all over America. We just don't read about or see these amazing images unless we are there making the images real.

It is amazing to think that a boy born in Mound Bayou, Mississippi, and raised in Memphis, can become the father of two successful classical musicians. This thought is very emotional for me.

I encourage you all to smile and cry as you watch your sons and daughters grow into successful men and women. Dads, you can also cry. Remember, we are human and are filled with emotion. Let it go. It's okay to show emotion, especially the positive kind. Be proud of the fact that you were there with your children, every step of the way.

Parents, you must start raising your children early in their lives. It starts from the day they are born and continues until they reach adulthood. What a joy it is to see my adult sons living their lives as positive and successful young men.

*McGill family.*

# Chapter Seventeen

## McGill's 25 Principles

The following are twenty-five principles Ira Carol and I used to raise and teach our sons. I am sure there are many other principles, guides, or teaching tools parents use, but these are the ones we concentrated on while raising our sons on the South Side of Chicago.

Some of you may recognize that your parents incorporated and used some of these same principles during their child-raising days. Understand that what works for one person or family may not work for you. Sift through the principles and choose ones that you feel comfortable with. I am sure that years from now or sooner, you will be writing your own principles–adding to the never ending keys parents across the world use to raise successful men and women.

## Key Principles For Raising Successful African American Men

1. Look at your child and say, "I Love you," at least once every day. Because of the stress put on you by outside forces, and even by your own son or daughter, you may not want to say these three powerful little words. Tell your child "I love you," regardless of how you feel at the moment.

2. All human beings need to be loved and touched. Give your child a strong hug and a kiss on the cheek, every day.

3. Don't be a drop-off parent. Be there during the parent and teacher meetings, music lessons, basketball games, swimming classes, and all of your child's activities. Children get satisfaction out of knowing their parents are sincerely concerned about their well-being and success while they are involved in activities, whether outside, or inside their home.

4. Before and after your child is born use every opportunity to teach. While in his mother's womb, his brain is functioning and responding to sounds. Do not think your child is incapable of learning at this young age. He is listening and learning.

5. Praise and compliment your children equally. Avoid sibling rivalry by not comparing siblings. They are individuals, and should be judged on their own merits.

6. Spend quality time with your child every day. Help him with homework assignments, and watch positive programs on television

together. Take him fishing at the local lake, to a little league base-ball game, museum, or a live concert or theater performance. Play old-fashioned board games and sports with him. Search your local newspapers to find free opportunities. Many museums have free days, and cultural centers have free activities and concerts. These fun and educational experiences will create an everlasting bond between you and your child.

7. Remove the television and computer from your child's bedroom. Place them in a common area of the house to monitor their use. Use Internet filters, or parental controls to block out sexual and violent content on the computer. Travel to faraway places with your child—by way of the Internet.

8. Find the best teachers. Good teachers will motivate your child and inspire him to want to learn. If necessary, seek the advice of friends, relatives, or other teachers, and understand that you should be your child's primary teacher.

9. Know your child's teachers, friends, and the friends' parents. Get telephone numbers and home and email addresses. Periodically communicate with them to establish an extended family of con-cerned parents, teachers, and friends.

10. Pick up your child after school if possible. This helps to ensure the child's safety. A photo of your child holding your hand while carrying his book bag will be an everlasting family treasure.

11. Recognize behavioral changes in your child, investigate causes, and take immediate action when necessary. In other words, "nip it in the bud." This prevents the issues or problems from growing into larger ones that might be difficult to manage.

12. Read to your child every day. Take him to a library and buy plenty of books. Visit used bookstores where you can find some low priced hidden treasures. You might also find that great classic at one of your local flea markets–for less than one dollar. During the summer months, explore outdoor book fairs, and don't neglect the indoor ones during winter. If possible, invest in a digital reader. Some are priced less than one hundred dollars. There are many Internet sites where you can download free books. Don't forget to buy some cloth books before your child starts to walk or talk. Most importantly, when he learns to read, have him read to you.

13. Find creative ways to reward your child for his accomplishments. Take him to see his favorite movie. Surprise him with a new pair of gym shoes, a new basketball, or a new book. Allow him to roam the aisles of a toy store and pick one or two of his favorite toys (within a certain price range).

14. Talk to your child. To teach, you must talk to him. Two-way communication is vital for you to get to know your child, and for him to get to know you. To understand what's going on in your child's mind, you must also be a good listener.

15. Don't let money be an issue. Your son's and daughter's success is worth every dollar. Take the necessary action to secure funding to support them. Take out a second mortgage if possible, or get a part time job. If you have a special skill, barter your service to pay for the music, dance, swimming, gymnastics, or science classes. Ira Carol once painted graphics on each side of Mr. Montgomery's school bus. In exchange, he transported Demarre from home to school and back for a full year.

16. Be at home with your child, especially during the infant and childhood stages of his life. A positive and loving home

environment can be a natural classroom for teaching. When a babysitter is needed, use family members or friends who share the same positive values as you.

17. Write encouraging letters or notes to your child. During the early years, these letters and notes can be used to teach reading and writing skills. In a short period of time, your child will be reading and writing to you. As he gets older, these letters and notes can be used to show your love and to motivate him to succeed.

18. Teach your child to establish goals early in his life. Ensure that the goals are written down and posted in the home, and on his computer and mobile phone. Let him know that goals can be changed periodically. Give your sons and daughters a special reward or treat each time they reach one of their goals.

19. Discipline your child when necessary, but don't ever use physical or mental violence as a disciplinary tool. Just as you found creative methods to reward your child for doing the right things, when it comes to discipline be just as creative.

20. Save your child's artwork, and other writings. Frame his drawings, paintings, and poems. Display them on the walls of your home. Displaying your child's creations helps to increase his self-esteem. Save all photographs and videos of your child. These gems will bring many smiles and tears of joy later in life.

21. Don't allow your child to say *I can't*. Teach him how he *can*. Constantly try to instill in your child's mind that he can reach all goals if he works hard and believes in himself.

22. Mental workouts are necessary for your child to succeed in school and the physical ones are just as important. Go to the park

and run. Play catch with a football or softball. Take long walks in safe areas. Sign him up to play organized team sports. This physical activity helps boys and girls develop strong bodies and minds.

23. To provide healthy foods and drinks for your child, and to identify harmful ingredients found in many popular foods, read ingredient labels found on the packaging of all grocery store foods. Limit the amount of sodium and sugar in your child's diet. Try not to eat or drink foods containing high fructose corn syrup, or other sweeteners like brown sugar syrup. Some food companies changed the name high fructose corn syrup to corn sugar. Many researchers have found these sweeteners to be harmful to humans. Foods with high amounts of trans fats should also be avoided. Avoid foods that are classified as genetically modified organisms (GMO). Do whatever is necessary to avoid childhood obesity by being a healthy role model for your child.

24. Teach your child to respect others. Teach him to have positive values. Teach him the meaning of the verse, "Do onto others as you would have them do unto you."

25. Be a positive role model for your child. Be his loudest cheerleader–at his school's holiday program, little league baseball game, music competition, or at the family bowling outing. Let him know through your actions that you care and want him to succeed, no matter what the endeavor. Parents who are raising a young child should begin to use these principles early in his life. Don't wait until he reaches a certain age–some principles can be used on the day he is born.

These twenty-five principles are not all encompassing, and I am sure, if you are serious about "raising your children well," your own principles will evolve. Your list of principles might even be more extensive than the ones listed here. Use whatever tools and guides that work for you.

*Brothers Anthony and Demarre McGill.*

Throughout this book, I sometimes used the words *he* and *him*, and the words *Raising Successful African American Men* are found in the title. It is important to remember that these principles can be used to raise all children, regardless of gender, race, ethnicity, or social class. The key is that you use them every day to, "raise them well."

# FURTHER READING ON RAISING SUCCESSFUL CHILDREN IN TOUGH CONTEMPORARY TIMES

*Gifted Hands: The Ben Carson Story,* by Ben Carson.

*Raising Black Children: Two Leading Psychiatrists Confront the Educational, Social, Emotional Problems Facing Black Children,* by James P. Comer and Alvin Poussaint.

*Raising African American Girls,* by Linda Ellis Eastman.

*Three Young Men Make a Pact and Fulfill a Dream,* by Sampson Davis.

*A Boy Should Know How to Tie a Tie: And Other Lessons for Succeeding in Life,* by Antwone Fisher.

*The Pursuit of Happyness,* by Chris Gardner.

*Raising Black Boys,* by Dr. Jawanza Kunjufu.

*Beating the Odds: Raising Academically Successful African American Males,* by Freeman Hrabowski, III, Kenneth Matson, and Goeffrey L. Grieb.

*Inner City Miracle,* by Judge Greg Mathis.

*Talkin' Back: Raising and Educating Resilient Black Girls,* by Dierdre Paul.

Dear De,

Your inner strength flows like the construction of a house. You are:

> the cement that holds the foundation together
> the mortar that glues the bricks in place
> the joist that bares the weight of the load
> the roof that shields the structure from outside elements.

A man of character <u>like you</u>, can do all these things and more because the depth of your love for family is limitless!

Happy Father's Day

Love,
Jill and Cassius
June 17, 2012

© Jill N. Trotter (a family friend for over four decades)

Made in the USA
Charleston, SC
31 July 2014